D0338596

The Seven Deadly Sins

Selected & Arranged by
Steven Schwartz

Foreword by
James Finn Garner

Gramercy Books
New York

This 2000 edition is published by Gramercy Books™, an imprint of Random House Value Publishing, Inc., 280 Park Avenue, New York, NY 10017, by arrangement with Macmillan Publishing USA.

Printed in the United States of America

Book design by Rachael McBrearty

Random House
New York • Toronto • London • Sydney • Auckland
http://www.randomhouse.com/

Library of Congress Cataloging-in-Publication Data

The seven deadly sins / selected and arranged by Steven Schwartz ; foreword by James Finn Garner.
p. cm.
ISBN 0-517-16208-3
1. Deadly sins--Quotations, maxims, etc. I. Schwartz, Steven, 1942-

PN6084.D39 S48 2000
241'.3--dc21

00-056202

8 7 6 5 4 3 2 1

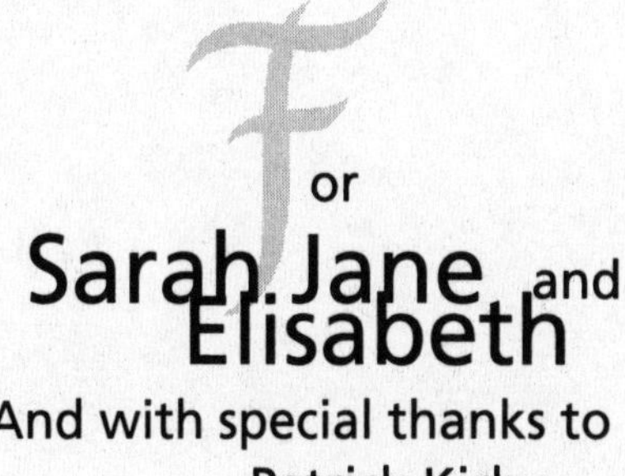

For
Sarah Jane and
Elisabeth

And with special thanks to
Patrick Kirby

Contents

He wrapped himself in quotations—as a beggar would enfold himself in the purple of Emperors.

Rudyard Kipling

Foreword

Sin? Ha! What an old-fashioned idea. This is the 1990s, after all. Unless you do something completely reprehensible, no one is likely to start screaming at you about archaic ideas like personal responsibility.

I don't mean to imply, though, that we're not fascinated by sin. We are. We love it. We can't hear enough about it—as long as we're talking about someone else. If these behavior categories are ever directed at ourselves, we most likely perform some glorious spin doctoring to dodge any blame.

Your own lust, for example, would be better described as "sensuality," especially if you live in California. Greed becomes "resource management optimization," or simply "takin' care of business." Anger, "being honest with your emotions." Pride would be "asserting your self-worth," while envy would be "fueling the spirit of healthy competition." After a day of such heavy rationalization, treat yourself to a few pints of Häagen-Dazs (gluttony) and kick back with some no-brainer personal time (sloth). And why not? You've earned it.

I found great reassurance in reading Steve Schwartz's compendium of carnal quotes and profane precepts. It was encouraging to be reminded that all these sinful tendencies have been with us from the beginning. Throughout all of human history, our actions and reactions have been fundamentally the same. From ancient Greece all the way to Hollywood U.S.A., we've deplored our weaknesses, surrendered to our baser selves, and savored the deliciousness of giving in. And then, the morning after, we've made the same half-hearted promises never, ever to stumble again. Now that you know you're helping maintain a long tradition, maybe you won't feel so bad next time you fall away from the straight and narrow.

Armies of pundits and preachers make a good living these days telling us that our society is in a horrible state of decay, and that people (especially the young!) are materialistic, lazy, short-tempered, and all the rest. But we always were, and probably always will be. Somehow, paradoxically, society is in a state of perpetual decline. In physics, this would be impossible; in human nature, it may be inevitable. There's some comfort to be taken in that.

So the next time you succumb to anger at someone's lame-brain driving, or sneak a peek at the "After Hours" movies on the hotel cable channel, or cast an envious glance at your neighbor's house, car, wife, hairline, or cholesterol count, turn to this handy book. If it doesn't quiet the protests of that small voice inside you that scolds you for your failings, at least it will give you some witty rejoinders to toss back.

James Finn Garner

Introduction

I love quotations because they don't make me wait. In a very few words, they can reveal a truth, provoke a laugh, or challenge a belief. They can confirm what I always knew, and startle me with a fresh way of seeing. There are quotes that inspire, reassure, and comfort; quotes that celebrate human aspirations for something greater, and quotes that exalt the everyday. And there's more. Quotes are constantly surprising: There are 2,500 year-old quotes that could have been written yesterday; quotes funny enough for the best comedy routines; and quotes from well-known people about unexpected subjects. (Example? Okay. How about *Davey Crockett* talking about *lust*—on page 194.)

Because quotes give me so much pleasure, I assembled this collection. *The Seven Deadly Sins* is not meant to be an exhaustive, definitive, final, all-there-is-to-know work; rather, it's a very personal sampling of snippets, excerpts, anecdotes—jokes, even—that grabbed me because they were moving, funny, or insightful . . . because the language was wonderful . . . because the person quoted was interesting . . . or because of the time the quote was written or said. Simply, these are the quotes that cost me money; quotes that inflated my phone bill with *Hey, listen to this!* calls to friends.

As an organizing principle, the sins themselves were very enticing. Nowhere else can you find every twist (and twisted) turn of human behavior examined, explored, and explained from such varied perspectives. Each of the seven is rich in its own way, so whether your feeling about sin is traditional and serious, modern and casual, or contemporary and whimsical—there's plenty here for you.

During the course of the research, I found myself expanding the category of each sin to include everything I found interesting: quotes that put a fresh spin on an old idea; quotes that offered a brand-new understanding; quotes that were *almost* about a sin; and quotes that were about its opposite.

Plus, I found an *additional* pile of quotes getting higher and harder to resist. So I included an eighth category: sin itself. In here went everything about the overall concept of sin; sins that didn't fit anywhere else; and, most important, sins the founding Church fathers couldn't even have *imagined*—a list that is either fascinating (and long) or depressing (and long) depending on your point of view. And speaking of the Church fathers, here's how the notion of the seven deadly sins came about in the first place.

There is no list of seven deadly sins in the Bible; the sins are in there, all right—but they're scattered around. The first actual *list* came out of the early Christian monastic tradition and contained the vices that would most seriously hamper a monk's spiritual growth. So even though it may seem strange that murder, stealing, or lying aren't represented, these simply weren't the everyday problems that pride, envy, anger, covetousness, gluttony, sloth, and lust were.

Although one could make a strong case for including some *other* human failings (like cowardice, vindictiveness, or cruelty), the counter-argument would be that *every* sin is a natural extension of the seven and, in fact, that the seven deadly sins aren't even sins at all—but tendencies in our character that *predispose* us to sin.

I had a great time researching this book; a time filled with chance discoveries, many laughs, provocative attitudes, and a continual admiration for the ability of some people to cut through all the *noise* and get directly to the heart of human experience.

So whether or not you agree with Susan Sontag that "the taste for quotations . . . is a surrealist taste," with Winston Churchill that "it is a good thing for an uneducated man to read books of quotations," with Guy Debord that "quotations are useful in periods of ignorance," or with Henry Fowler that "pretentious quotations [are] the surest road to tedium," I think everyone can agree with Jorge Luis Borges, who summed it all up by saying, "Life itself is a quotation."

Steven Schwartz, New York City, 1997

Sin
Lust Covetousn
Anger
Envy
Covet
Gluttony
Lust
Sloth
Pride Covetousn
Gluttony Anger
Pride
Sin
Lust
Covet
Pride Envy
Sin
Lust
Pride
Anger
Gluttony
Envy
Pride
Covetousness
Anger
Lust
Envy
Pride
Lust
Envy
Covetousness
Anger
Gluttony

Sin

Sin: Sin

Definition: (sin), *n.* 1. willful or deliberate violation of some religious or moral principle 2. any reprehensible action or behavior 3. serious fault

See: evil; immorality; vileness; transgression; iniquity; weakness; debauchery; indecency; wickedness; corruption; lewdness; obscenity; profligacy; imperfection; enticement; temptation; seduction; deficiency; smuttiness; vice; shortcoming; infraction; flaw; debility; immoderation; attraction; fascination; damnation; misdeed; offense; peccability; venality; impropriety; feebleness; wrongdoing; misconduct; debt; violation; error; imperfection; demerit; entrapment; disobedience; insobriety; unchastity; wantonness; promiscuity; shamelessness; impudence; defilement; exhibitionism; coarseness; grossness; nastiness; ribaldry; bawdry; salaciousness; dirt; filth; intemperance; hedonism; prurience; voyeurism; scopophilia; indulgence; unrestraint; frailty; indelicacy

See also: err; transgress; bait; lure; trespass; appeal; charm; backslide; cheat; deviate; lapse; misbehave; captivate; offend; stray; fail; entice; wander; breach; trap; fall; prostitute; slip; tempt; relapse; stumble; have flaws; fall from grace; sow wild oats; live in sin; do misdeeds; go astray; lose one's innocence; wallow in the mire; do wrong; have moral turpitude; be at fault; be brazen; be loose; be immodest; be wicked; be fast; be wayward; be whorish; be willful; be ungodly; be carnal; be a degenerate; fix; snort; mainline; shoot up; hit up; skin pop; pill pop; chase the dragon; freebase; smoke dope; trip

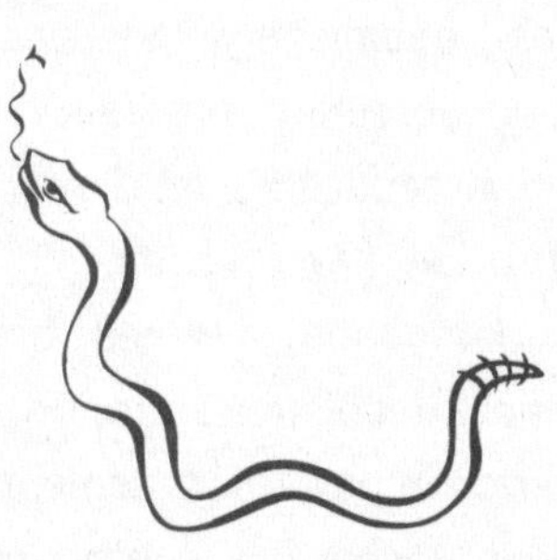

The seven deadly sins . . . food, clothing, fire, rent, taxes, respectability and children.

George Bernard Shaw (1856–1950), Irish playwright, author, critic

Caesarius of Heisterbach, a Cistercian monk and medieval chronicler, tells of a Cistercian lay brother who was heard to pray to Christ: "Lord, if Thou free me not from this temptation, I will complain of Thee to Thy mother."

Will Durant (1885–1981), American editor and author

Christ died for your sins. Dare we make his martyrdom meaningless by not committing them?

Jules Feiffer (b. 1929), American cartoonist and writer

You get a better class of person at orgies, because people have to keep in trim more. There is an awful lot of going round holding in your stomach, you know. Everybody is very polite to each other. The conversation isn't very good but you can't have everything.

Gore Vidal (b. 1925), American novelist and playwright

If there is any larceny in a man—golf will bring it out.

Paul Gallico (1897–1976), American novelist

He neither drank, smoked, nor rode a bicycle. Living frugally, saving his money, he died early, surrounded by greedy relatives. It was a great lesson to me.

John Barrymore (1882–1942), American actor

Sin is a dangerous toy in the hands of the virtuous. It should be left to the congenitally sinful, who know when to play with it and when to let it alone.

H.L. Mencken (1880–1956), American satirist and editor

He has not a single redeeming defect.

Benjamin Disraeli (1804–1881), English prime minister and author

Wolves which batten upon lambs, lambs consumed by wolves, the strong who immolate the weak, the weak victims of the strong: there you have Nature, there you have her intentions, there you have her scheme: a perpetual action and reaction, a host of vices, a host of virtues, in one word, a perfect equilibrium resulting from the equality of good and evil on earth.

Marquis de Sade (1740–1814), French author

Excess on occasion is exhilarating. It prevents moderation from acquiring the deadening effect of habit.

W. Somerset Maugham (1874–1965), English novelist and playwright

The hottest places in Hell are reserved for those who, in times of great moral crisis, maintain their neutrality.
Dante Alighieri (1265–1321), Italian poet

How drab and empty life would be without these sins, and what dull dogs we would all be without a healthy trace of many of them in our make up! And has not the depiction of these sins and their consequences been the yeast in most fiction and drama? Could Shakespeare, Voltaire, Balzac, Dostoevski, or Tolstoy have written their masterpieces if humanity had been innocent of these sins? It is almost as if Leonardo, Titian, Rembrandt and Van Gogh had been required to paint without using any primary colours.
Ian Fleming (1908–1964), English novelist

Somewhere, and I can't find where, I read about an Eskimo hunter who asked the local missionary priest, "If I did not know about God and sin, would I go to hell?" "No," said the priest, "not if you did not know." "Then why," asked the Eskimo earnestly, "did you tell me?"
Annie Dillard (b. 1945), American writer and naturalist

The passions are the only orators which always persuade.
Duc François de la Rochefoucauld (1613–1680), French author

Jupiter, not wanting man's life to be wholly gloomy and grim, has bestowed far more passion than reason—you could reckon the ratio as twenty-four to one. Moreover, he confined reason to a cramped corner of the head and left the rest of the body to the passions.
Desiderius Erasmus (1466?–1536), Dutch scholar

A great many people have come up to me and asked how I manage to get so much work done and still keep looking so dissipated.
Robert Benchley (1889–1945), American humorist

Everything one does in life, even love, occurs in an express train racing toward death. To smoke opium is to get out of the train while it is still moving. It is to concern oneself with something other than life or death.
Jean Cocteau (1889–1963), French poet, novelist, and film director

I've over-educated myself in all the things I shouldn't have known at all.
Noël Coward (1899–1973), English actor and playwright

My problem lies in reconciling my gross habits with my net income.
Errol Flynn (1909–1959), English-born American film actor

Who loves not wine, woman and song,
Remains a fool his whole life long.

Martin Luther (1483–1546), German religious reformer

Everyone is dragged on by their favorite pleasure.

Virgil (70–19 B.C.), Roman poet

All the things I really like to do are either illegal, immoral, or fattening.

Alexander Woollcott (1887–1943), American journalist

They had been corrupted by money, and he had been corrupted by sentiment. Sentiment was the more dangerous, because you couldn't name its price. A man open to bribes was to be relied upon below a certain figure, but sentiment might uncoil in the heart at a name, a photograph, even a smell remembered.

Graham Greene (1904–1991), English author

He [Sir Walter Raleigh] took a pipe of tobacco a little before he went to the scaffold, which some formal persons were scandalized at, but I think 'twas well done and properly done, to settle his spirits.

John Aubrey (1626–1697), English writer

I am not over-fond of resisting temptation.

William Beckford (1760–1844), eccentric English dilettante and author

"You oughtn't to yield to temptation." "Well, somebody must, or the thing becomes absurd," said I.

Sir Anthony Hope Hawkins (1532–1595), English naval commander

Do you really think it is weakness that yields to temptations? I tell you that there are terrible temptations which it requires strength, strength and courage, to yield to.

Oscar Wilde (1854–1900), Irish poet, wit, and playwright

There is not any memory with less satisfaction than the memory of some temptation we resisted.

James Branch Cabell (1879–1958), American novelist and essayist

Is this her fault or mine?
The tempter or the tempted, who sins most?

William Shakespeare (1564–1616), English playwright and poet

God forgive me, I do still see that my nature is not to be quite conquered, but will esteem pleasure above all things; though, yet in the middle of it, it hath reluctancy after my business, which is neglected by my fallowing my pleasure. However, music and women I cannot but give way to, whatever my business is.

Samuel Pepys (1633–1703), English diarist

They declaim against the passions without bothering to think that it is from their flame philosophy lights its torch.
Marquis de Sade (1740–1814), French author

The Methodists love your big sinners, as proper subjects to work upon.
Horace Walpole (1717–1797), English author

I am a bad, wicked man, but I am practising moral self-purification; I don't eat meat any more, I now eat rice cutlets.
Vladimir Lenin (1870–1924), Russian Communist leader

There is a book that says we're all sinners, and I at least chose a sin that's made quite a few people happier than they were before they met me, a sin that's left me with very little time to consider extremely popular moral misdemeanors, like usury, intolerance, bearing false tales, extortion, racial bigotry, and casting the first stone.
Sally Stanford (1903–1982), American madam and writer

I've made so many movies playing a hooker that they don't pay me in the regular way anymore. They leave it on the dresser.
Shirley MacLaine (b. 1934), American actor and writer

For art to exist, for any sort of aesthetic activity or perception to exist, a certain physiological precondition is indispensable: intoxication.
Friedrich Nietzsche (1844–1900), German philosopher and poet

It is the hour to be drunken! To escape being the martyred slaves of time, be ceaselessly drunk. On wine, on poetry, or on virtue, as you wish.
Charles Baudelaire (1821–1867), French poet

True debauchery is liberating because it creates no obligations. If you possess only yourself; hence it remains the favorite pastime of the great lovers of their own person.
Albert Camus (1913–1960), French existentialist writer

Let's not quibble! I'm the foe of moderation, the champion of excess. If I may lift a line from a die-hard whose identity is lost in the shuffle, "I'd rather be strongly wrong than weakly right."
Tallulah Bankhead (1903–1968), American film actor

If Jupiter hurled his thunderbolt as often a man sinned, he would soon be out of thunderbolts.
Ovid (43 B.C.–A.D. 17), Roman poet

The Anglo-Saxon conscience does not prevent the Anglo-Saxon from sinning; it merely prevents him from enjoying his sin.
Salvador de Madariaga y Rojo (1886–1978), Spanish author and diplomat

We record our solemn judgment that the habitual use of tobacco is a practice out of harmony with the best Christian life.
The Doctrines and Discipline of the Methodist Episcopal Church, 1932

Conscience: the inner voice which warns us that someone may be looking.
H. L. Mencken (1880–1956), American satirist and editor

Man is the Only Animal that Blushes. Or needs to.
Mark Twain (1835–1910), American humorist

When choosing between two evils, I always take the one I've never tried before.
Mae West (1893–1980), American film actor

Of two evils choose the prettier.
Carolyn Wells (1862–1942), American author

If you resolve to give up smoking, drinking and loving, you don't actually live longer; it just seems longer.
Clement Freud (b. 1924), English politician and writer

Things forbidden have a secret charm.
Tacitus (55?–120?), Roman orator, politician, and historian

It is the function of vice to keep virtue within reasonable bounds.
Samuel Butler (1835–1902), English author

The follies which a man regrets most, in his life, are those which he didn't commit when he had the opportunity.
Helen Rowland (1875–1950), American journalist

The only way to get rid of a temptation is to yield to it. Resist it, and your soul grows sick with longing for the things it has forbidden to itself.
Oscar Wilde (1854–1900), Irish poet, wit, and playwright

It is easier to denature plutonium than to denature the evil spirit of man.
Albert Einstein (1879–1955), German-born American physicist

If the world were merely seductive, that would be easy. If it were merely challenging, that would be no problem. But I rise in the morning torn between a desire to improve (or save) the world and a desire to enjoy (or savour) the world. This makes it hard to plan the day.
E. B. White (1899–1985), American author

What is morality in any given time or place? It is what the majority then and there happen to like, and immorality is what they dislike.
Alfred North Whitehead (1861–1947), English mathematician and philosopher

Obscenity is whatever gives a Judge an erection.
Anonymous

Take me, I am the drug; take me, I am hallucinogenic.
Salvador Dalí (1904–1989), Spanish painter

Lead me not into temptation. I can find the way myself.
Rita Mae Brown (b. 1944), American writer and playwright

Wickedness is a myth invented by good people to account for the curious attractiveness of others.
Oscar Wilde (1854–1900), Irish poet, wit, and playwright

It is so stupid of modern civilization to have given up believing in the devil when he is the only explanation of it.
Ronald Knox (1888–1957), English theologian and essayist

A hick town is one in which there is no place to go where you shouldn't be.
Alexander Woollcott (1887–1943), American journalist

You should make the point of trying every experience once—except incest and folk-dancing.
Anonymous

Why not seize the pleasure at once? How often is happiness destroyed by preparation, foolish preparation!
Jane Austen (1775–1817), English novelist

There is no moral precept that does not have something inconvenient about it.
Denis Diderot (1713–1784), French philosopher

Sara could commit adultery at one end and weep for her sins at the other, and enjoy both operations at once.
Arthur Joyce Lunel Cary (1888–1957), English novelist

Ugliness is a sin.
Frank Lloyd Wright (1867–1959), American architect

The biggest sin is sitting on your ass.
Florynce Kennedy (b. 1916), American lawyer and civil rights activist

There's only one real sin, and that is to persuade oneself that the second-best is anything but the second-best.
Doris Lessing (b. 1919), English writer

The only sin is mediocrity.
Martha Graham (1893–1991), American dancer, teacher, and choreographer

Near our vineyard there was a pear tree laden with fruit that was not attractive in either flavor or form. One night, when I (at the age of sixteen) had played until dark on the sandlot with some other juvenile delinquents, we went to shake that tree and carry off its fruit. From it we carried off huge loads, not to feast on, but to throw to the pigs, although we did eat a few ourselves. We did it just because it was forbidden.

Saint Augustine (354–430), Church father and philosopher

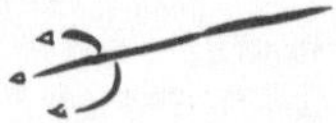

I don't hate homosexuals. I love homosexuals. It's the sin of homosexuality I hate.

Anita Bryant (b. 1940), American singer

But . . . don't you feel a little guilty when somebody catches you looking at one of those fold-out pictures in the "men's" magazines? Don't you blush slightly when you're discovered reading *My Awful Confessions* or some mag like that? Don't you hesitate to mention that you saw *I Was a Teenage Sexpot!* at the movie last night? I *hope* you hesitate, and blush, and feel guilty . . . if so there's still hope for ya!

Pat Boone (b. 1934), American singer

The biggest temptation is . . . to settle for too little.

Thomas Merton (1915–1968), American author and Trappist monk

I try never to be alone with a beautiful woman. Because when I'm alone, the devil in me becomes dangerous.

Tiny Tim (1922–1996), American singer and entertainer

Evil comes from the darkness of women.

Antonin Artaud (1896–1948), French dramatist, poet, and surrealist

It is odd that neither the Church nor modern public opinion condemns petting, provided it stops short at a certain point. At what point sin begins is a matter to which causists differ. One eminently orthodox Catholic divine laid it down that a confessor may fondle a nun's breasts, provided he does it without evil intent. But I doubt whether modern authorities would agree with him on this point.

Bertrand Russell (1872–1970), English philosopher

The world is round. Only one-third of the human beings are asleep at one time, and the other two-thirds are awake and up to some mischief somewhere.

Dean Rusk (1909–1994), American statesman and secretary of state

So far, about morals, I know only that what is moral is what you feel good after and what is immoral is what you feel bad after.
Ernest Hemingway (1899–1961), American author

Every sin is the result of a collaboration.
Stephen Crane (1871–1900), American author

I am an atheist still, thank God.
Luis Buñuel (1900–1983), Spanish filmmaker

In some sort of crude sense which no vulgarity, no humour, no overstatement can quite extinguish, the physicists have known sin; and this is a knowledge which they cannot lose.
J. Robert Oppenheimer (1904–1967), American physicist

The world has achieved brilliance without wisdom, power without conscience. Ours is a world of nuclear giants and ethical infants.
Omar Bradley (1893–1981), American general

The means by which we live have outdistanced the ends for which we live. Our scientific power has outrun our spiritual power. We have guided missiles and misguided men.
Martin Luther King Jr. (1929–1968), American civil rights leader

The prince of darkness is a gentleman.
William Shakespeare (1564–1616), English playwright and poet

The only thing necessary for the triumph of evil is for good men to do nothing.
Edmund Burke (1729–1797), Irish statesman, orator, and philosopher

Whoever fights monsters should see to it that in the process he does not become a monster. And when you look long into the abyss, the abyss also looks into you.
Friedrich Nietzsche (1844–1900), German philosopher and poet

Do what you will.
Francois Rabelais (1490–1553), French humorist and satirist

Never practice two vices at once.
Tallulah Bankhead (1903–1968), American film actor

Never support two weaknesses at the same time. It's your combination sinners—your lecherous liars and your drunkards—who dishonor the vices and bring them into bad repute.
Thornton Wilder (1897–1975), American author and playwright

Thou hast the keys of Paradise, O just, subtle and mighty opium.
Thomas De Quincey (1785–1859), English author

Really to sin you have to be serious about it.
Henrik Ibsen (1828–1906), Norwegian poet and playwright

Of course heaven forbids certain pleasures, but one finds means of compromise.
Molière (1622–1673), French actor and playwright

Once a woman has forgiven her man, she must not reheat his sins for breakfast.
Marlene Dietrich (1901?–1992), German-born American film actor

Be sober, be vigilant; because your adversary, the Devil, as a roaring lion, walketh about seeking whom he may devour.
The New Testament, I Peter 5:8

It's all right letting yourself go, as long as you can get yourself back.
Mick Jagger (b. 1943), English rock musician.

Let the good times roll.
Cajun motto

Whenever you are to do a thing, though it can never be known but to yourself, ask yourself how you would act were all the world looking at you, and act accordingly.
Thomas Jefferson (1743–1826), third American president

You must pay for your sins. If you have already paid, please ignore this notice.
Sam Levenson (1911–1980), American author and humorist

When our first parents were driven out of Paradise, Adam is believed to have remarked to Eve: "My dear, we live in an age of transition."
Dean William Ralph Inge (1860–1954), English Anglican prelate, scholar, and author

Evils in the journey of life are like the hills which alarm travelers on the road. Both appear great at a distance, but when we approach them we find they are far less insurmountable than we had conceived.
Charles Caleb Colton (1780–1832), English Anglican clergyman

Our sins, like our shadows when day is in its glory, scarce appear; toward evening, how great and monstrous they are!
Sir John Suckling (1609–1642), English poet

Gambling is the child of avarice, the brother of iniquity, and the father of mischief.

George Washington (1732–1799), first American president

One of the greatest triumphs of the nineteenth century was to limit the connotation of the word "immoral" in such a way that, for practical purposes, only those were immoral who drank too much or made too copious love. Those who indulged in any or all of the older deadly sins could look down in righteous indignation on the lascivious and the gluttons.

Aldous Huxley (1894–1963), English author

Every human being who is conceived by the coition of a man with a woman is born with original sin, subject to impiety and death, and therefore a child of wrath.

Gratian (367–383), Roman Christian emperor

If we come into the World infected and depraved with sinful Disposition, then Sin must be natural to us; and if natural, then necessary; and if necessary, then no Sin.

John Taylor (1580–1653), English author

Saint: *n.* A dead sinner, revised and edited.

Ambrose Bierce (1842–1914), American writer

Other men's sins are before our eyes; our own are behind our back.

Lucius Annaeus Seneca (3 B.C.?–A.D. 65?), Roman statesman and philosopher

I always claim the mission workers came out too early to catch any sinners on this part of Broadway. At such an hour the sinners are still in bed resting up from their sinning of the night before, so they will be in good shape for more sinning a little later on.

Damon Runyon (1884–1946), American journalist and author

Lady Peabury was in the morning room reading a novel; early training gave a guilty spice to this recreation, for she had been brought up to believe that to read a novel before luncheon was one of the gravest sins it was possible for a gentlewoman to commit.

Evelyn Waugh (1903–1966), English author

The way of the adulterer is hedged with thorns; full of fears and jealousies, burning desires and impatient waitings, tediousness of delay and sufferance of affronts, and amazements of discovery.

Jeremy Taylor (1613–1667), English churchman and author

If a man lie with the wife of another man at her wish there shall be no penalty for him. As for the woman, her husband shall punish her as he pleases.
The Assyrian Code

Men never do evil so completely and cheerfully as when they do it from religious conviction.
Blaise Pascal (1623–1662), French scientist and philosopher

An Englishman thinks he is moral when he is only uncomfortable.
George Bernard Shaw (1856–1950), Irish playwright, author, and critic

A cap of good acid costs five dollars and for that you can hear the Universal Symphony with God singing solo and the Holy Ghost on drums.
Hunter S. Thompson (b. 1939), American writer

The best pleasures of this world are not quite pure.
Johann Wolfgang von Goethe (1749–1832), German poet and philosopher

Prostitutes are a necessity. Without them, men would attack respectable women in the streets.
Napoleon Bonaparte (1769–1821), French emperor

The perfect hostess will see to it that the works of male and female authors be properly separated on her book shelves. Their proximity, unless they happen to be married, should not be tolerated.
Lady Gough (nineteenth century), English author

He said he was against it.
Calvin Coolidge (1872–1933), thirtieth American president, after being asked what had been said by a clergyman who had preached on sin

For thy sake, tobacco, I
Would do any thing but die.
Charles Lamb (1775–1834), English essayist and critic

Herein is not only a great vanity, but a great contempt of God's good gifts, that the sweetness of man's breath, being a good gift of God, should be willfully corrupted by this stinking smoke.
James I of England (James VI of Scotland), (1566–1625)

No one ever reached the worst of a vice at one leap.
Juvenal (47–138), Roman lawyer and satirist

O Lord, if there is a Lord, save my soul, if I have a soul.
Joseph Ernest Renan (1823–1892), French historian

Nobody talks so constantly about God as those who insist that there is no God.

Heywood Broun (1888–1939), American journalist and author

Your wickedness makes you, as it were, heavy as lead, and to tend downwards with great weight and pressure towards Hell; and if God should let you go, you would immediately sink and swiftly descend and plunge into the bottomless gulf, and your healthy constitution, and your own care and prudence, and best contrivance, and all your righteousness, would have no more influence to uphold you and keep you out of Hell than a spider's web would have to stop a falling rock.

Jonathan Edwards (1703–1758), American Congregational clergyman and theologian

An atheist is a man who has no invisible means of support.

Sir John Buchan (1875–1940), Scottish author and governor general of Canada

God is merciful and men are bribable, and that's how his will is done on earth as it is in Heaven. Corruption is our only hope. As long as there's corruption, there'll be merciful judges and even the innocent may get off.

Bertolt Brecht (1898–1956), German poet and playwright

There are crimes which become innocent and even glorious through their splendour, number, and excess.

Duc François de la Rochefoucauld (1613–1680), French author

An improper mind is a perpetual feast.

essayist

His face was filled with broken commandments.

John Masefield (1878–1967), English poet and playwright

An apology for the devil: It must be remembered that we have only heard one side of the case. God has written all the books.

Samuel Butler (1835–1902), English author

We may not pay Satan reverence, for that would be indiscreet, but we can at least respect his talents.

Mark Twain (1835–1910), American humorist

A belief in a supernatural source of evil is not necessary; man alone is quite capable of every wickedness.

Joseph Conrad (1857–1924), Ukraine-born English novelist

It is a sin to believe evil of others, but it is seldom a mistake.

H. L. Mencken (1880–1956), American satirist and editor

I'll die young, but it's like kissing God.

Lenny Bruce (1926–1966), American comedian, on drugs

So far as we are human, what we do must be either evil or good: so far as we do evil or good, we are human: and it is better, in a paradoxical way, to do evil than to do nothing: at least we exist.

T. S. Eliot (1888–1965), American-born English poet and critic

It is a curious thing that every creed promises a paradise which will be absolutely uninhabitable for anyone of civilized taste.

Evelyn Waugh (1903–1966), English author

I hold it to be the inalienable right of anybody to go to hell in his own way.

Robert Frost (1874–1963), American poet

Heresy is only another word for freedom of thought.

Graham Greene (1904–1991), English author

It makes a great difference whether a person is unwilling to sin, or does not know how.

Lucius Annaeus Seneca (3? B.C.–A.D. 65?), Roman statesman and philosopher

Many are saved from sin by being so inept at it.

Mignon McLaughlin (b. 1930), American writer

There are only two sorts of men: the one the just, who believe themselves sinners; the other sinners, who believe themselves just.

Blaise Pascal (1623–1662), French scientist and philosopher

Should we all confess our sins to one another we would all laugh at one another for lack of originality.

Kahlil Gibran (1883–1931), Lebanese poet and painter

A private sin is not so prejudicial in the world as a public indecency.

Miguel de Cervantes (1547–1616), Spanish novelist painter

Original sin is in us, like the beard. We are shaved to-day and look clean, and have a smooth chin; to-morrow our beard has grown again, nor does it cease growing while we remain on earth. In like manner original sin cannot be extirpated from us; it springs up in us as long as we live. Nevertheless we are bound to resist it to our utmost strength, and to cut it down unceasingly.

Martin Luther (1483–1546), German religious reformer

The devil tempted Christ, but it was Christ who tempted the devil to tempt him.

Samuel Butler (1835–1902), English author

Man-like is to fall into sin; fiendlike it is to dwell therein.

Henry Wadsworth Longfellow (1807–1882), American poet

Never open the door to a lesser evil, for other and greater ones invariably slink in after it.

Baltasar Gracian (1601–1658), Spanish writer and Jesuit priest

It has been my experience that folks who have no vices have very few virtues.

Abraham Lincoln (1809–1865), sixteenth American president

I prefer a comfortable vice to a virtue that bores.

Molière (1622–1673), French actor and playwright

Why don't you sin a little? Doesn't God deserve to have something to forgive you for?

Martin Luther (1483–1546), German religious reformer

I know a man who gave up smoking, drinking, sex, and rich food. He was healthy right up until the time he killed himself.

Johnny Carson (b. 1925), American comedian

One big vice in a man is apt to keep out a great many smaller ones.

Bret Harte (1836–1902), American writer

Some men flee from temptation, but others just crawl away from it hoping it will overtake them.

Anonymous

He has all the virtues I dislike, and none of the vices I admire.

Winston Churchill (1874–1965), English prime minister and author

It's a sort of curious phenomenon that God is somehow not quite as nice as the devil; the devil doesn't punish you for behaving well, but God punishes you for behaving badly.

Jacob Bronowski (1908–1974), Polish-born English historian and mathematician

In the desert, an old monk had once advised a traveler, the voices of God and the Devil are scarcely distinguishable.

Loren Eiseley (1907–1977), American anthropologist and writer

Show me a community or a country where all the minor vices are discouraged and I will show you one bereft of major virtues.

Heywood Broun (1888–1939), American journalist and author

Life in itself is neither good nor evil; it is the scene of good or evil, as you make it.

Michel Eyquem de Montaigne (1533–1592), French essayist

One is always wrong to open a conversation with the devil, for, however he goes about it, he always insists upon having the last word.

André Gide (1869–1951), French author and critic

It is not opium which enables me to work, but its absence; and to feel its absence it must from time to time pass through me.

Antonin Artaud (1896–1948), French dramatist, poet, and surrealist

Only the opium eater truly understands the pain of death.

John Cheever (1912–1982), American writer

There were sins that were too subtle to be explained, and there were others that were too terrible to be clearly mentioned. For example, there was sex, which was always smouldering just under the surface and which suddenly blew up into a tremendous row when I was about twelve.

George Orwell (1903–1950), American writer

We tolerate without rebuke the vices with which we have grown familiar.

Publilius Syrus (first century B.C.), Roman poet and actor

Sins cannot be undone, only forgiven.

Igor Stravinsky (1882–1971), Russian-born American composer

Astronomy was born of superstition; eloquence of ambition, hatred, falsehood, and flattery; geometry of avarice; physics of an idle curiosity; and even moral philosophy of human pride. Thus the arts and sciences owe their birth to our vices.

Jean-Jacques Rousseau (1712–1778), French philosopher

As for an authentic villain, the real thing, the absolute, the artist, one rarely meets him even once in a lifetime. The ordinary bad hat is always in part a decent fellow.

Colette (1873–1954), French writer

It is an open question whether any behavior based on fear of eternal punishment can be regarded as ethical or should be regarded as merely cowardly.

Margaret Mead (1901–1978), American anthropologist and author

One becomes moral as soon as one is unhappy.

Marcel Proust (1871–1922), French novelist

Watch and pray, that ye enter not into temptation: the spirit indeed is willing, but the flesh is weak.

The New Testament, Matthew 26:41

The world loves a spice of wickedness.

Henry Wadsworth Longfellow (1807–1882), American poet

Christianity gave eroticism its savor of sin and legend when it endowed the human female with a soul.
Simone de Beauvoir (1908–1986), French writer

Forsaking egoism, power, pride, lust, anger and possession; freed from the notion of "mind," and tranquil; one is thus fit to become one with Brahman.
"The Bhagavad-Gita" (fifth century B.C.), Sanskrit poem

Sick and perverted always appeals to me.
Madonna (b. 1959), American singer and actor, on pornography

No monster vibration, no snake universe hallucinations. Many tiny jeweled violet flowers along the path of a living brook that looked like Blake's illustration for a canal in grassy Eden: huge Pacific watery shore, Orlovsky dancing naked like Shiva long-haired before giant green waves, titanic cliffs that Wordsworth mentioned in his own Sublime, great yellow sun veiled with mist hanging over the planet's oceanic horizon. No harm.
Allen Ginsberg (1926–1997), American poet, describing an LSD trip

Nothing enchants the soul so much as young women. They alone are the cause of evil, and there is no other.
Bharitihari (first century A.D.), Indian grammarian

Meanwhile the passions rage like tyrants, and throw into confusion the whole soul and life of men with storms from every quarter, fear on one side, desire on another, on another anxiety, or false empty joy, here pain for the thing which was loved and lost, there eagerness to win what was not possessed, there grief for an injury received, here burning desire to avenge it. Wherever he turns, avarice can confine him, self-indulgence dissipate him, ambition master him, pride puff him up, envy torture him, sloth drug him, obstinacy rouse him, oppression afflict him, and the countless other feelings which crowd and exploit the power of passion.
Saint Augustine (354–430), Church father and philosopher

Laughter does not seem to be a sin, but it leads to sin.
St. John Chrysostom (345?–407), father of the Greek church

Art is vice. One does not wed it, one rapes it.
Edgar Degas (1834–1917), French artist

We are most unfair to God: we do not allow him to sin.
Friedrich Nietzsche (1844–1900), German philosopher and poet

That there is a devil is a thing doubted by none but such as are under the influence of the Devil. For any to deny the being of a Devil must be from ignorance or profaneness worse than diabolical.
Cotton Mather (1663–1728), American Congregational minister

Vice is its own reward.
Quentin Crisp (b. 1908), English author

It is impossible to repent of love. The sin of love does not exist.
Muriel Spark (b. 1918), English writer

Nothing evil was created by God; we ourselves have produced all the wickedness.
Tatian (second century A.D.), Syrian-Christian apologist and heretic

If only there were evil people somewhere insidiously committing evil deeds and it were necessary only to separate them from the rest of us and destroy them. But the line dividing good and evil cuts through the heart of every human being. And who is willing to destroy a piece of his own heart?
Alexander I. Solzhenitsyn (b. 1918), Russian writer

Men may commit theft as well as adultery with the eye.
Xenocrates of Chalcedon (396–314 B.C.), Greek philosopher

Women, Priests, and Poultry have never enough.
Thomas Fuller (1608–1661), English clergyman

The gods can either take away evil from the world and will not; or they neither can nor will, or lastly, they are both able and willing. If they have the will to remove the evil and cannot, then they are not omnipotent. If they can, but will not, then they are not benevolent. If they are neither able nor willing, then they are neither omnipotent nor benevolent. Lastly, if they are both able and willing to annihilate evil, how does it exist?
Epicurus (341–270 B.C.), Greek philosopher

The problem of evil. . . . Why does God permit it? Or, if God is omnipotent, in which case permission and creation are the same, why did God create it?
Sir William Temple (1881–1944), archbishop of Canterbury

The only reason that cocaine is such a rage today is that people are too dumb and lazy to get themselves together to roll a joint.

Jack Nicholson (b. 1937), American film actor

She [The Catholic Church] holds that it were better for sun and moon to drop from heaven, for the earth to fail, and for all the many millions who are upon it to die of starvation in extremist agony, as far as temporal affliction goes, than that one soul, I will not say, should be lost, but should commit one single venial sin, should tell one willful untruth . . . or steal one poor farthing without an excuse.

Cardinal John Henry Newman (1801–1890), English Catholic leader

Tobacco had nowhere been forbidden in the Bible, but then it had not yet been discovered. . . . St. Paul would almost certainly have condemned tobacco if he had known of its existence. . . . It was possible [though] that God knew Paul would have forbidden smoking, and had purposely arranged the discovery of tobacco for a period at which Paul should no longer be living. This might seem rather hard on Paul, considering all he had done for Christianity, but it would be made up to him in other ways.

Samuel Butler (1835–1902), English author

What were once vices are now the manners of the day.

Lucius Annaeus Seneca (3? B.C.– A.D. 65?), Roman statesman and philosopher

Never tell a loved one of an infidelity; you would be badly rewarded for your trouble. Although one dislikes being deceived, one likes even less being undeceived.

Ninon de Lenclos (1620–1705), French society figure

A drug is neither moral or immoral—it's a chemical compound. The compound itself is not a menace to society until a human being treats it as if consumption bestowed a temporary license to act like an asshole.

Frank Zappa (1940–1993), American rock musician

And when I saw my devil, I found him serious, thorough, profound, solemn: He was the spirit of gravity—through him all things fall.

Friedrich Nietzsche (1844–1900), German philosopher and poet

I met the Devil last night. It was exactly three minutes past midnight. He said: "After all, what does it matter whether you write it or not? Why not go to bed?"

Christopher Morley (1890–1957), American author

An old lady in church was seen to bow whenever the name Satan was mentioned. One day the minister met her and asked why she did so. "Well," she replied, "politeness costs nothing—and you never know."
Anonymous

Our young contemporaries do not wish to suffer or grow pale; on the contrary, they have a most determined desire to grow pink and enjoy themselves. But too much enjoyment "blunts the fine point of seldom pleasure." Unrestrained indulgence kills not merely passion, but, in the end, even amusement.
Aldous Huxley (1894–1963), English author

It is the restrictions placed on vice by our social code which make its pursuit so peculiarly agreeable.
Kenneth Grahame (1859–1932), Scottish writer

The incompensable value of giving free reign to one's vices consists in this, that they rise into view in all their strength and size, even if, in the excitement of indulgence, one catches only a faint glimpse of them. One doesn't learn to be a sailor by exercising in a puddle, though too much training in a puddle can probably render one unfit to be a sailor.
Franz Kafka (1883–1924), Czech-born Austrian author

Never let your morals get in the way of doing what's right.
Isaac Asimov (1920–1982), American writer

There are three ways a man can be ruined: women, gambling, and farming. My father chose the most boring.
Pope John XXIII (1882–1963)

The problem with people who have no vices is that generally you can be pretty sure they're going to have some pretty annoying virtues.
Elizabeth Taylor (b. 1932), English-born American film star

I always said to people that society consists of two forces fighting one another, good and evil. There's talent on both sides, but there's more talent on the side of evil. Make no mistake. They hire the best brains, the best people.
Alex Rose (1898–1976), New York Liberal Party leader

You're mistaken if you think wrong doers are always unhappy. The really professional evil-doers love it. They're happy as larks in the sky . . . . The unhappy ones are only the guilty amateurs and the neurotics.
Muriel Spark (b. 1918), English writer

I don't say we ought to misbehave, but we ought to look as if we could.

Orson Welles (1915–1985), American actor, writer, and filmmaker

It is difficult to live without opium after having known it because it is difficult . . . to take the earth seriously. And unless one is a saint, it is difficult to live without taking the earth seriously.

Jean Cocteau (1889–1963), French poet, novelist, and film director

Sin has always been an ugly word, but it has been made so in a new sense over the last half-century. It has been made not only ugly but passé. People are no longer sinful, they are only immature or underprivileged or frightened or, more particularly, sick,

Phyllis McGinley (1905–1978), American poet and author

For God's sake, if you sin, take pleasure
in it,
And do it for the pleasure.

Gerald Gould (1885–1936), English poet

Sins become more subtle as you grow older: You commit sins of despair rather than lust.

Piers Paul Read (b. 1941), English author

I count religion but a childish toy,
And hold there is no sin but ignorance.

Christopher Marlowe (1564–1593), English playwright

I always say beauty is only sin deep.

Saki (1870–1916), Scottish writer and wit

The road of excess leads to the palace of wisdom.

William Blake (1757–1827), English artist, poet, and mystic

I like extravagance. Letters which give the postman a stiff back to carry, books which overflow from their covers, sexuality which bursts the thermometer.

Anaïs Nin (1903–1977), French novelist and diarist

One's condition on marijuana is always existential. One can feel the importance of each moment and how it is changing one. One feels one's being, one becomes aware of the enormous apparatus of nothingness—the hum of a hi-fi set, the emptiness of a pointless interruption, one becomes aware of the war between each of us, how the nothingness in each of us seeks to attack the being of others, how our being is in turn attacked by the nothingness in others.

Norman Mailer (b. 1923), American writer

Scenes of passion ... should not be introduced when not essential to the plot ... In general, passion should be so treated that these scenes do not stimulate the lower and baser elements.
Motion Picture Producers and Distributors Code, March 31, 1930

The trouble with incest is that it gets you involved with relatives.
George S. Kaufman (1889–1961), American playwright

If everybody in this town connected with politics had to leave town because of [chasing women] and drinking, you'd have no government.
Barry Goldwater (b. 1909), American politician

There are three side effects of acid. Enhanced long-term memory, decreased short-term memory and I forgot the third.
Timothy Leary (1920–1996), American scientist and writer

Pride
Lust Sloth
Anger
Envy Pride
Covetousness
Gluttony
Anger
Lust
Envy
Sin
Lust
Pride
Gluttony
Gluttony Anger
Lust Sloth Envy
Sloth Sin
Pride
Sin
Lust
Covetousness
Envy
Sloth
Pride Envy Covetousness Anger
Envy
Sin
Sin
Anger
Gluttony
Envy
Pride
Sin
Sloth

pride

Sin: Pride

Definition: (prīd), *n.* a high or inordinate opinion of one's own dignity, importance, merit, or superiority, whether as cherished in the mind or as displayed in bearing, conduct, and so on

See: self-esteem; arrogance; conceit; self-love; braggadocio; egotism; self-congratulation; presumptuousness; huffiness; impertinence; indifference; hubris; me-ism; stand-offishness; immodesty; high-handedness; vanity; haughtiness; snobbery; elitism; self-respect; gravity; solemnity; reserve; detachment; self-centeredness; propriety; stateliness; distinction; presence; pomposity; audacity; vainglory; impudence; narcissism; self-praise; hollowness; insolence; hauteur; contempt; aloofness; assumption; big-headedness; cockiness; superbity;

self-importance; contumely; loftiness; overconfidence; smugness; pretension; superciliousness; self-applause; grandiosity; self-glorification; self-admiration

See also: boast; patronize; swagger; flaunt; crow; prance; exult; vaunt; gasconade; swell; overbear; plume; disdain; condescend; strut; revel in; have a swelled head; love oneself; glory in; hold one's head high; put on airs; flatter oneself; lord it over; be stuck up; be snooty; be swank; be brazen; be on a high horse; be bumptious; be puffed up; be hoity-toity; be elevated; be starchy; be uppity; be high and mighty; be unabashed; be noble; be royal; be kingly; be majestic; be aristocratic; be lordly; be unblushing; be overbearing

One of my chief regrets during my years in the theater is that I couldn't sit in the audience and watch me.
John Barrymore (1882–1942), American actor

To love oneself is the beginning of a lifelong romance.
Oscar Wilde (1854–1900), Irish poet, wit, and playwright

An actor's a guy who, if you ain't talking about him, ain't listening.
Marlon Brando (b. 1924), American actor

You can pick out actors by the glazed look that comes into their eyes when the conversation wanders away from themselves.
Michael Wilding (1912–1979), English actor

"The ego is hateful," you say. Not mine. I should have liked it in another; should I be hard to please because it is mine?
André Gide (1869–1951), French author and critic

Diogenes came to Plato's house one day and was disgusted to find rich and exquisite carpets on the floor. To show his contempt he stomped and wiped his feet on them, saying, "Thus do I trample upon the pride of Plato."

"With greater pride," observed Plato mildly.
As recounted by Clifton Fadiman (b. 1904), American author and editor

Early in life I had to choose between honest arrogance and hypocritical humility. I chose honest arrogance and I have seen no occasion to change.
Mark Twain (1835–1910), American writer

What I chiefly desire for you is a genuine full-blooded egoism, which shall force you for a time to consider the thing that concerns you as the only thing of consequence and everything else as non-existent. Now don't take this wish as something brutal in my nature! There is no way you can benefit society more than by coining the metal that you know is yourself.
Henrik Ibsen (1828–1906), Norwegian poet and playwright

The longer I live the more I see that I am never wrong about anything, and that all the pains that I have so humbly taken to verify my notions have only wasted my time.
George Bernard Shaw (1856–1950), Irish playwright, author, and critic

I may have faults, but being wrong ain't one of them.
Jimmy Hoffa (1913–1975), American labor leader

If horses could paint they would draw gods like horses.
Xenophanes (570–475 B.C.), Greek philosopher

He who despises himself nevertheless esteems himself as a self-despiser.
Friedrich Nietzsche (1844–1900), German philosopher and poet

Don't be humble. You're not that great.
Golda Meir (1898–1978), Israeli prime minister, said to General Moshe Dayan

She invents dramas in which she always stars.
Anaïs Nin (1903–1977), American novelist and diarist

Wounded vanity knows when it is mortally hurt; and limps off the field, piteous, all disguises thrown away. But pride carries its banner to the last; and as fast as it is driven from one field it unfurls it in another.
Helen Hunt Jackson (1830–1885), American author

The last time I saw him he was walking down Lovers' Lane holding his own hand.
Fred Allen (1894–1956), American humorist

Every author, however modest, keeps a most outrageous vanity chained like a madman in the padded cell of his breast.
Logan Pearsall Smith (1865–1946), American essayist

The most difficult secret for a man to keep is his own opinion of himself.
Marcel Proust (1871–1922), French novelist

No poet or novelist wishes he were the only one who ever lived, but many of them wish they were the only one alive, and quite a number believe their wish has been granted.
W. H. Auden (1907–1973), English poet

The longer I'm out of office, the more infallible I appear to myself.
Henry Kissinger (b. 1923), American secretary of state

I made them *see*, didn't I. . . I changed everything. Remember how small the world was before I came along. I made them see it both ways, in time as well as space. . . I brought it all to life. I moved the whole world onto a twenty foot screen.
D.W. Griffith (1875–1948), American film director

We grow tired of everything but turning others into ridicule and congratulating ourselves on their defects.
William Hazlitt (1778–1830), English essayist and critic

The proud hate pride—in others.

statesman, scientist, and writer

He that tooteth not his own horn, the same shall not be tooted.
John L. Lewis (1880–1969), American labor leader, said to his children

As soon as there were two, there was pride.
John Donne (1573–1631), English poet

Some conjurors say that number three is the magic number, and some say number seven. It's neither, my friend, neither. It's number one.
Charles Dickens (1812–1870), English novelist

Pride is generally censured and decried, but mainly by those who have nothing to be proud of.
Arthur Schopenhauer (1788–1860), German philosopher

If I cannot brag of knowing something, then I brag of not knowing it; at any rate, brag.
Ralph Waldo Emerson (1803–1882), American essayist and poet

My family pride is something inconceivable. I can't help it. I was born sneering.
W. S. Gilbert (1836–1911), English librettist

Humility is not my forte, and whenever I dwell for any length of time on my own shortcomings, they gradually begin to seem mild, harmless, rather engaging little things, not at all like the staring defects in other people's characters.
Margaret Halsey (b. 1910), American writer

If I only had a little humility, I would be perfect.
Ted Turner (b. 1938), American entertainment executive

He was like a cock who thought the sun had risen to hear him crow.
George Eliot (1819–1880), English novelist

There, but for the grace of God, goes God.
Herbert J. Mankiewicz (1897–1953) American screenwriter and journalist, said of Orson Welles; also attributed to others

Well, not bad, but there are decidedly too many of them, and they are not very well arranged. I should have done it differently.
James McNeill Whistler (1834–1903), American painter, when asked if he agreed that the stars were especially beautiful one night

We are so vain that we even care for the opinion of those we don't care for.
Marie von Ebner-Eschenbach (1830–1916), Austrian novelist and poet

In defeat unbeatable: in victory unbearable.
Winston Churchill (1874–1965), English prime minister and author, referring to Viscount Montgomery

No man thinks there is much ado about nothing when the ado is himself.
Anthony Trollope (1815–1882), English novelist

At home I am a nice guy: But I don't want the world to know. Humble people, I've found, don't get very far.
Muhammad Ali (b. 1942), American boxing champion

I really do not see much use in exalting the humble and meek; they do not remain humble and meek long when they are exalted.
Samuel Butler (1835–1902), English author

A narcissist is someone better looking than you are.
Gore Vidal (b. 1925), American novelist and playwright

I dote on myself, there is that lot of me and all so luscious.
Walt Whitman (1819–1892), American poet

I have little patience with anyone who is not self-satisfied. I am always pleased to see my friends, happy to be with my wife and family, but the high spot of every day is when I first catch a glimpse of myself in the shaving mirror.
Robert Morley (1908–1992), English actor and playwright

We can bear to be deprived of everything but our self-conceit.
William Hazlitt (1778–1830), English essayist and critic

Here we may reign secure, and in my choice
To reign is worth ambition though in hell:
Better to reign in hell than serve in heaven.
John Milton (1608–1674), English poet

Many a man is praised for his reserve and so-called shyness when he is simply too proud to risk making a fool of himself.
J. B. Priestley (1894–1984), English novelist, critic, and playwright

The advantage of doing one's praising for oneself is that one can lay it on so thick and exactly in the right places.
Samuel Butler (1835–1902), English author

The French want no-one to be their *superior*. The English want *inferiors*. The Frenchman constantly raises his eyes above him with anxiety. The Englishman lowers his beneath him with satisfaction. On either side it is pride, but understood in a different way.
Alexis de Tocqueville (1805–1859), French historian

Those who believe that they are exclusively in the right are generally those who achieve something.
Aldous Huxley (1894–1963), English author

Whatever talents I possess may suddenly diminish or suddenly increase. I can with ease become an ordinary fool. I may be one now. But it doesn't do to upset one's own vanity.
Dylan Thomas (1914–1953), Welsh poet

A *proper* pride is a necessity to an artist in any of the arts. Only this will save an artist's work and his private life from the attacks and intrusions made on these by those unfortunate persons who have been unable to attract attention to themselves except by incessant bawling.
Edith Sitwell (1887–1964), English poet, critic, and novelist

Just as it is always said of slander that something always sticks when people boldly slander, so it might be said of self-praise (if it is not entirely shameful and ridiculous) that if we praise ourselves fearlessly, something will always stick.
Francis Bacon (1561–1626), English philosopher and author

I know I'm not clever but I'm always right.
J. M. Barrie (1860–1937), Scottish novelist and playwright

Self-love for ever creeps out, like a snake, to sting anything which happens . . . to stumble upon it.
Lord Byron (1788–1824), English poet

Self-love is often rather arrogant than blind; it does not hide our faults from ourselves, but persuades us that they escape the notice of others.
Samuel Johnson (1709–1784), English author

If some really acute observer made as much of egotism as Freud has made of sex, people would forget a good deal about sex and find the explanation for everything in egotism.
Wallace Stevens (1879–1955), American poet

Fame is a powerful aphrodisiac.
Graham Greene (1904–1991), English author

The man who believes he can live without others is mistaken; and the man who thinks others can't live without him is even more mistaken.
Hasidic saying

An author, like any other so-called artist, is a man in whom the normal vanity of all men is so vastly exaggerated that he finds it a sheer impossibility to hold it in. His overpowering impulse is to gyrate before his fellow men, flapping his wings and emitting defiant yells. This being forbidden by the police of all civilized nations, he takes it out by putting his yells on paper. Such is the thing called self-expression.
H. L. Mencken (1880–1956), American satirist and editor

The vain poet is of the opinion that nothing of his can be too much: he sends to you basketful after basketful of juiceless fruit, covered with scentless flowers.
Walter Savage Landor (1175–1864), English author

I often quote myself. It adds spice to my conversation.
George Bernard Shaw (1856–1950), Irish playwright, author, and critic

I'm no different from anybody else with two arms, two legs, and forty-two hundred hits.
Pete Rose (b. 1942), American baseball star

They charged me with the commission of great crimes; but men of my stamp do not commit crimes.
Napoleon Bonaparte (1769–1821), French emperor

Pomposity is only the failure of pomp.
G. K. Chesterton (1874–1936), English journalist and author

He is by all odds the most interesting man he ever knew.
Leo Rosten (b. 1908), American humorist

Conceit is God's gift to little men.
Bruce Barton (1886–1967), American advertising executive and author

One of the surprising things of this world is the respect a worthless man has for himself.
Edgar Watson Howe (1853–1937), American editor and author

There are few people who are more often in the wrong than those who cannot endure to be thought so.
Duc François de La Rochefoucauld (1613–1680), French author

Whenever nature leaves a hole in a person's mind, she generally plasters it over with a thick coat of self-conceit.

Henry Wadsworth Longfellow (1807–1882), American poet

When Providence wishes to destroy the small, it does so by putting big words into their little mouths.

Sir Rabindranath Tagore (1861–1941), Bengali poet

What is the first business of philosophy? To part with self-conceit. For it is impossible for any one to begin to learn what he thinks that he already knows.

Epictetus (A.D. 55?–135?), Greek philosopher

People wrapped up in themselves never unfold.

Puzant Kevork Thomajan (b. 1902), American author and poet

Pride may be allowed to this or that degree, else a man cannot keep up his dignity. In gluttony there must be eating, in drunkenness there must be drinking; 'tis not the eating, and 'tis not the drinking that must be blamed, but t he excess. So in pride.

John Selden (1584–1654), English jurist and statesman

Pride counterbalances all our miseries, for it either hides them, or if it discloses them, boasts of that disclosure. Pride has such a thorough possession of us, even in the midst of our miseries and faults, that we are prepared to sacrifice life with joy, it if may but be talked of.

Blaise Pascal (1623–1662), French scientist and philosopher

According to Christian teachers, the essential vice, the utmost evil, is Pride. Unchastity, anger, greed, drunkenness, and all that, are mere flea-bites in comparison: It was through Pride that the devil became the devil: Pride leads to every other vice: It is the complete anti-God state of mind.

C. S. Lewis (1898–1963), English literary scholar and novelist

Self-love is a cup without any bottom, you might pour all the Great Lakes into it, and never fill it up.

Oliver Wendell Holmes (1841–1935), American jurist

[Pride] is a case of mistaken nonentity.

Barbara Stanwyck (1907–1990), American actor

I never wonder to see men wicked, but I often wonder to see them not ashamed.

Jonathan Swift (1667–1745), Anglo-Irish author

Vanity is the more odious and shocking to everybody, because everybody, without exception, has vanity; and two vanities can never love one another.
Lord Chesterfield (1694–1773), English statesman

Praise shames me, for I secretly beg for it.
Sir Rabindranath Tagore (1861–1941), Bengali poet

Apology is only egotism wrong side out.
Oliver Wendell Holmes (1841–1935), American jurist

Nothing soothes our vanity as a display of greater vanity in others; it makes us vain, in fact, of our modesty.
Louis Kronenberger (1904–1980), American critic, editor, and author

To say that a man is vain merely means that he is pleased with the effect he produces on other people. A conceited man is satisfied with the effect he produces on himself.
Max Beerbohm (1872–1956), English critic and caricaturist

He who denies his own vanity usually possesses it in so brutal a form that he instinctively shuts his eyes to avoid the necessity of despising himself.
Friedrich Nietzsche (1844–1900), German philosopher and poet

Why do men seek honor? Surely, in order to confirm the favorable opinion they have formed of themselves.
Aristotle (384–322 B.C.), Greek philosopher

Those who know the least of others think the highest of themselves.
Charles Caleb Colton (1780–1832), English Anglican clergyman

It is the nature of extreme self-lovers, as they will set a house on fire, and it were but to roast their eggs.
Francis Bacon (1561–1626), English philosopher and author

Talk about conceit as much as you like, it is to human character what salt is to the ocean; it keeps it sweet, and renders it endurable.
Oliver Wendell Holmes (1841–1935), American jurist

Conceit is the finest armour a man can wear.
Jerome K. Jerome (1859–1927), English humorist, playwright, and novelist

What, will the world be quite overturned when you die?
Epictetus (A.D. 55?–135?), Greek stoic philosopher

The sun will set without thy assistance.
The Talmud

A sick man that gets talking about himself, a woman that gets talking about her baby, and an author that begins reading out of his own book, never know when to stop.
Oliver Wendell Holmes (1841–1935), American jurist

We would rather speak badly of ourselves than not at all.
Duc François de La Rochefoucauld (1613–1680), French author

Simple narcissism gives the power of beasts to politicians, professional wrestlers, and female movie stars.
Norman Mailer (b. 1923), American writer

One must learn to love oneself . . . with a wholesome and healthy love, so that one can bear to be with oneself and need not roam.
Friedrich Nietzsche (1844–1900), German philosopher and poet

His eminence was due to the flatness of the surrounding landscape.
John Stuart Mill (1806–1873), English philosopher and economist

A modest man is morally admired—if people ever hear of him.
Edgar Watson Howe (1853–1937), American editor and author

He [Turgenev] had the air of his own statue erected by national subscription.
Oliver Wendell Holmes (1841–1935), American jurist

I am better than my reputation.
Friedrich von Schiller (1759–1805), German poet and playwright

A confessional passage has probably never been written that didn't stink a little bit of the writer's pride in having given up his pride.
J. D. Salinger (b. 1919), American author

I do not believe that any peacock envies another peacock his tail, because every peacock is persuaded that his own tail is the finest in the world. The consequence of this is that peacocks are peaceable birds.
Bertrand Russell (1872–1970), English philosopher

[Pride is the] only trip. You are who you are because of your ego.
John Cassavetes (1929–1989), American actor and film director

He is a self-made man who worships his creator.
John Bright (1811–1889), English orator and statesman, on Benjamin Disraeli

Change in fashion is the tax which the industry of the poor levies on the vanity of the rich.
Nicolas Chamfort (1741–1794), French author

Modesty: The gentle art of enhancing your charm by pretending not to be aware of it.
Oliver Herford (1863–1935), English author and illustrator

I like the moment when I break a man's ego.
Bobby Fischer (b. 1943), American chess champion

The most difficult secret for a man to keep is his own opinion of himself.
Marcel Pagnol (1895–1974), French playwright, screenwriter, and film director

He's the type of man who will end up dying in his own arms.
Mamie Van Doren (b. 1933), American actor, on Warren Beatty

Whatever women do they must do twice as well as men to be thought half as good. Luckily this is not difficult.
Charlotte Whitton (1896–1975), Canadian politician and writer, on becoming mayor of Ottawa

I was born for soccer, just as Beethoven was born for music.
Pelé (b. 1940), Brazilian soccer player

I arrived in Hollywood without having my nose fixed, my teeth capped, or my name changed. That is very gratifying to me.
Barbra Streisand (b. 1942), American singer, drector, and actor

In my early days I was a sepia Hedy Lamarr. Now I'm black and a woman, singing my own way.
Lena Horne (b. 1917), American singer and actor

Everybody wants to be Cary Grant. Even I want to be Cary Grant.
Cary Grant (1904–1996), English-born American film actor

I don't read books, I write them.
Henry Kissinger (b. 1923), American secretary of state, when asked if he had read a current bestseller

I'm an instant star. Just add water and stir.
David Bowie (b. 1947), English rock singer

They gave me star treatment when I was making a lot of money. But I was just as good when I was poor.
Bob Marley (1945–1981), Jamaican reggae singer

I pride myself on the fact that my work has no socially redeeming value.
John Waters (b. 1946), American film director

I have no use for humility. I am a fellow with an exceptional talent.

Jackie Gleason (1916–1987), American comedian and actor

I have a memory like an elephant. In fact, elephants often consult me.

Noël Coward (1899–1973), English actor and playwright

Sometimes I amaze myself. I say this humbly.

Don King (b. 1931), American boxing promoter

I am just too much.

Bette Davis (1908–1989), American film actor

My problem is intense vanity and narcissism. I've always had such a good physique and such intense charm that it's difficult to be true to myself.

Lawrence Durrell (b. 1912–1990), Anglo-Irish novelist, poet, and playwright

I can hold a note as long as the Chase National Bank.

Ethel Merman (1904–1984), American Broadway star

I've known all my life I could take a bunch of words and throw them up in the air and they would come down just right. I'm a semantic Paganini.

Truman Capote (1924–1984), American writer and playwright

I'm the most translated writer in the world, behind Lenin, Tolstoy, Gorki and Jules Verne. And they're all dead.

Mickey Spillane (b. 1918), American writer

I've outdone anyone you can name—Mozart, Beethoven, Bach, Strauss, Irving Berlin, he wrote 1,001 tunes. I wrote 5,500.

James Brown (b. 1928), American blues and rock singer

I am the hero of Africa.

Idi Amin (b. 1925), Ugandan dictator

I was France.

Charles de Gaulle (1890–1970), French general and president

I know the Haitian people because I *am* the Haitian people.

François ("Papa Doc") Duvalier (1907–1971), Haitian dictator

There was never yet a true orator or poet who thought anyone better than himself.

Cicero (106–43 B.C.), Roman orator and philosopher

I like to be introduced as America's foremost actor. It saves the necessity of further effort.

John Barrymore (1882–1942), American actor

All my shows are great. Some of them are bad. But they're all great.

Lew Grade (b. 1906), English theatrical impresario

People hate me because I am a multifaceted, talented, wealthy, internationally famous genius.

Jerry Lewis (b. 1926), American actor and comedian

I've been through it all, baby. I'm Mother Courage.

Elizabeth Taylor (b. 1932), American film actor

Nobody can be exactly like me. Sometimes even I have trouble doing it.

Tallulah Bankhead (1903–1968), American actor

I was the originator, I was the emancipator, I was the architect of rock 'n' roll. And didn't nobody want to give me credit for it. I didn't ask anybody for it because I just made it up and I didn't think—it's just like if you're barefoot and you make yourself a pair of shoes. When I made rock 'n' roll I got tired of the old people's music of that time. I did it because that's what I wanted to hear. I was tired of the slow music.

Little Richard (b. 1935), American rock-and-roll singer

Caesar, when he first went into Gaul, made no scruple to profess "that he would rather be first in a village in Gaul than second in Rome."

Francis Bacon (1561–1626), English philosopher, quoting Julius Caesar

I have discovered the dance. I have discovered the art which has been lost for two thousand years.

Isadora Duncan (1878–1927), American dancer

I do not believe . . . I know.

Carl Jung (1875–1961), Swiss psychiatrist

I am sufficiently proud of my knowing something to be modest about my not knowing everything.

Vladimir Nabokov (1899–1977), Russian-born American novelist and poet

If I'm a lousy writer, a helluva lot of people have got lousy taste.

Grace Metalious (1924–1964), American novelist

I never realized until lately that women were supposed to be the inferior sex.

Katharine Hepburn (b. 1909), American actor

If I have to, I can do anything. I am strong, I am invincible, I am woman.

Helen Reddy (b. 1941), Australian-born American singer and songwriter

Why does the blind man's wife paint herself?
Benjamin Franklin (1706–1790), American statesman, scientist, and author

Caesar or nothing.
Cesare Borgia (1476?–1507), Italian cardinal and military leader

Ah, but a man's reach should exceed his grasp,
Or what's a heaven for?
Robert Browning (1812–1889), English poet

Ambition . . .
The glorious fault of angels and of gods.
Alexander Pope (1688–1744), English poet

Ambition, old as mankind, the immemorial weakness of the strong.
Vita Sackville-West (1892–1962), English novelist, poet, and critic

Vanity of vanities, saith the preacher, vanity of vanities: all is vanity.
The Old Testament, Ecclesiastes 1:2

Pride ruined the angels.
Ralph Waldo Emerson (1803–1882), American essayist and poet

None are more taken in by flattery than the proud who wish to be first and are not.
Baruch Spinoza (1632–1677), Dutch philosopher

I never wanted to be a crumb. If I had to be a crumb, I'd rather be dead.
Salvatore "Lucky" Luciano (1897–1962), Sicilian-born American gangster

Vanity is only being sensitive to what other people probably think of us.
Paul Valéry (1871–1945), French poet and philosopher

Hew not too high,
Lest the chips fall in thine eye.
Fourteenth-century English proverb

Never yield to that temptation, which to most young men, is very strong, of exploring other people's weaknesses and infirmities, or of showing your own superiority. You may get the laugh on your side by it, for the present; but you will make enemies by it for ever; and even those who laugh with you then, will, upon reflection, fear, and consequently hate you: besides that, it is ill-natured, and that a good heart desires rather to conceal, than expose, other people's weaknesses or misfortunes. If you have wit, use it to please, and not to hurt. You may shine, like the sun in temperate zones, without scorching.
Lord Chesterfield (1694–1773), English statesman

The ring always believes that the finger lives for it.
Malcolm de Chazal (1902–1981), French writer

Do not get excited over the noise you have made.
Desiderius Erasmus (1466?–1536), Dutch scholar

Whatever you may be sure of, be sure of this: that you are dreadfully like other people.
James Russell Lowell (1819–1891), American poet, essayist,and diplomat

Let us be a little humble; let us think that the truth may not perhaps be entirely with us.
Jawaharlal Nehru (1889–1964), Indian prime minister

If you want to be respected by others the great thing is to respect yourself. Only by that, only by self-respect will you compel others to respect you.
Fyodor Dostoevski (1821–1881), Russian novelist

One never dives into the water to save a drowning man more eagerly than when there are others present who dare not take the risk.
Friedrich Nietzsche (1844–1900), German philosopher and poet

The most silent people are generally those who think most highly of themselves.
William Hazlitt (1778–1830), English essayist and critic

Let's climb up the top of our ivory tower, right up to the last step, close to the heavens!
Gustave Flaubert (1821–1880), French novelist

A man who is not a fool can rid himself of every folly but vanity.
Jean-Jacques Rousseau (1712–1778), Swiss-born French philosopher and author

Those who write against vanity want the glory of having written well, and their readers the glory of reading well, and I who write this have the same desire, as perhaps those who read this have also.
Blaise Pascal (1623–1662), French scientist and philosopher

Pride is to character, like the attic to the house . . . the highest part, and generally the most empty.
John Gay (1685–1732), English poet and playwright

She was a human duck off whose back even the most searing of words flowed like harmless rain.
H. E. Bates (1905–1974), English author

Vanity may be likened to the smooth-skinned and velvet-footed mouse, nibbling about forever in expectation of a crumb.

William Gilmore Simms (1806–1870), American author

When I was young my vanity was such that when I went to a brothel I always picked the ugliest girl and insisted on making love to her in front of them all without taking my cigar out of my mouth. It wasn't any fun for me: I just did it for the gallery.

Gustave Flaubert (1821–1880), French novelist

Women have served all these centuries as looking-glasses possessing the magic and delicious power of reflecting the figure of man at twice its natural size.

Virginia Woolf (1882–1941), English author

Every man regards his own life as the New Year's Eve of time.

Jean Paul Richter (1763–1825), German novelist and humorist

Pride thinks its own happiness shines the brighter, by comparing it with the misfortunes of other persons. . . . This is that infernal serpent that creeps into the breasts of mortals.

Sir Thomas More (1478–1535), English statesman and author

Immodest creature, you do not want a woman who will accept your faults, you want one who pretends that you are faultless—one who will caress the hand that strikes her and kiss the lips that lie to her.

George Sand (1804–1876), French author

There is perhaps no one of our natural passions so hard to subdue as *pride*. Disguise it, struggle with it, beat it down, stifle it, mortify it as much as one pleases, it is still alive, and will every now and then peep out and show itself.

Benjamin Franklin (1706–1790), American statesman, scientist, and author

I liked your opera. I think I will set it to music.

Ludwig van Beethoven (1770–1827), German composer, to a fellow composer

So in your discussions of the nuclear freeze proposals, I urge you to beware the temptation of pride—the temptation blithely to declare yourselves above it all and label both sides equally at fault, to ignore the facts of history and the aggressive impulses of an evil empire, to simply call the arms race a giant misunderstanding and thereby remove yourself from the struggle between right and wrong, good and evil.

Ronald Reagan (b. 1911), American actor and fortieth president

Nobody has done anything to develop the English language since Shakespeare except myself, and Henry James perhaps a little.

Gertrude Stein (1874–1946), American expatriate writer

Take away the self-conceited, and there will be elbow-room in the world.

Benjamin Whichcote (1609–1683), English theologian

I am very willing to admit that I have some poetical abilities.

Robert Burns (1759–1796), Scottish poet

I do not object to Gladstone's always having the ace of trumps up his sleeve, but only to his pretence that God had put it there.

Henry Labouchere (1831–1912), English journalist and politician

How men long for celebrity! Some would willingly sacrifice their lives for fame, and not a few would rather be known by their crimes than not known at all.

Sir John Sinclair (1754–1835), Scottish writer

Some people, when they hear an echo, think they originated the sound.

Ernest Hemingway (1899–1961), American author

Baloney is flattery so thick it cannot be true; blarney is flattery so thin we like it.

Fulton J. Sheen (1895–1979), American Roman Catholic bishop and author

I suppose flattery hurts no one, that is, if he doesn't inhale.

Adlai Stevenson (1900–1965), American politician

Tell me what you brag about and I'll tell you what you lack.

Spanish proverb

I am ready to meet my *Maker*. Whether my *Maker* is prepared for the ordeal of meeting me is another matter.

Sir Winston Churchill (1874–1965), English prime minister and author

This is the epitaph I want on my tomb: "Here lies one of the most intelligent animals who ever appeared on the face of the earth."

Benito Mussolini (1883–1945), Italian dictator

It is best to act with confidence, no matter how little right you have to it.

Lillian Hellman (1905–1984), American playwright and memorist

To have that sense of one's intrinsic worth which constitutes self-respect is potentially to have everything.

Joan Didion (b. 1934), American writer

Immense power is acquired by assuring yourself in your secret reveries that you were born to control affairs.

Andrew Carnegie (1835–1919), American steel magnate

I always thought I should be treated like a star.

Madonna (b. 1958), American pop singer and actor

"Glamour" is assurance. It is a kind of knowing that you are all right in every way, mentally and physically and in appearance, and that, whatever the occasion or the situation, you are equal to it.

Marlene Dietrich (1901–1992) German-born American film actor

I want to do it because I want to do it.

Amelia Earhart (1897–1937), American aviator

I wish it, I command it. Let my *will* take the place of a reason.

Juvenal (60?–130?) Roman lawyer and satirist

But enough of me. Let's talk about you. What do you think of me?

Ed Koch (b. 1924), mayor of New York

So why talk about it? We don't have time to talk about something that's not about me!

Elisabeth Schwartz (b. 1980), student

Are there any writers on the literary scene whom I consider truly great? Yes, Truman Capote. But there are others who while not quite in this exalted orbit, are still commemorable.

Truman Capote (1924–1984), American writer and playwright

H. L. Mencken suffers from the hallucination that he is H. L. Mencken—there is no cure for a disease of that magnitude.

Maxwell Bodenheim (1892–1954), American poet and writer

I could readily see in [Ralph Waldo] Emerson . . . a gaping flaw. It was the insinuation that had he lived in those days, when the world was made, he might have offered some valuable suggestions.

Herman Melville (1819–1891), American author

The way Bernard Shaw believes in himself is very refreshing in these atheistic days when so many people believe in no God at all.

Israel Zangwill (1864–1926), English writer and playwright

My vanity is excessive: wherever I sit is the head of the table.

H. L. Mencken (1880–1956), American satirist and editor

I married beneath me, all women do.

Lady Nancy Astor (1879–1964), English politician (first woman member of Parliament)

An ass chosen to carry the statue of Isis, before which the people kneeled in reverence, thought the homage was paid to him.

G. C. Lichtenberg (1742–1799), German physicist and writer

Pryde, the general root of all harmes; for of this root springen . . . Ire, Envye, Accidie or Sloth, Avarice, Glotonye and Lecherye.

Geoffrey Chaucer (1343?–1400), English author

There is no crevice so small or intricate at which our self-love will not contrive to creep in.

William Hazlitt (1778–1830), English essayist and critic

Many a man is praised for his reserve and so-called shyness when he is simply too proud to risk making a fool of himself.

J. B. Priestley (1894–1984), English novelist, critic, and playwright

Man has always sacrificed truth to his vanity, comfort and advantage. He lives by make-believe.

W. Somerset Maugham (1874–1965), English novelist and playwright

Avoid having your ego so close to your position that when your position falls, your ego goes with it.

Colin Powell (b. 1937), American military leader

I have never made but one prayer to God, a very short one: "O Lord, make my enemies ridiculous." And God granted it.

Voltaire (1694–1778), French author

You've no idea of what a poor opinion I have of myself, and how little I deserve it.

W. S. Gilbert (1836–1911), English librettist

I can write better than anybody who can write faster, and I can write faster than anybody who can write better.

A. J. Liebling (1904–1963), American writer

Give me a museum and I'll fill it.

Pablo Picasso (1881–1973), Spanish artist

I would have made a good Pope.

Richard M. Nixon (1913–1994), thirty-seventh American president

I have too great a soul to die like a criminal.

John Wilkes Booth (1838–1865), American actor and assassin of Abraham Lincoln

Before feminism was, Paglia was!

Camille Paglia (b. 1947), American writer

The greatest of all faults, I should say, is to be conscious of none.
Thomas Carlyle (1765–1881), English author

The human being's first duty . . . is to think about himself until he has exhausted the subject, then he is in a condition to take up minor interests and think of other people.
Mark Twain (1835–1910), American humorist

He was so conceited it was beneath his dignity even to talk to himself.
Shalom Aleichem (1859–1916), Russian-born American humorist

I've got sagging breasts and a low-slung ass . . . but I can still get men.
Edith Piaf (1915–1963), French singer

Don't accept your dog's admiration as conclusive evidence that you are wonderful.
Ann Landers (b. 1918), American advice columnist

Modesty is a virtue not often found among poets, for almost every one of them thinks himself the greatest in the world.
Miguel de Cervantes (1547–1616), Spanish novelist

[Pride is an] amiable illusion, which the shape of our planet prompts, that every man is at the top of the world.
Ralph Waldo Emerson (1803–1882), American essayist and poet

Love yourself first and everything else falls into line. You really have to love yourself to get anything done in this world.
Lucille Ball (1911–1989), American comedian (attributed to others)

There were some initial difficulties when the director first told me the disappointing news that if the film were to have semblance of reality at all there would have to be moments when other people were on screen at the same time I was.
Bette Midler (b. 1945), American singer and actor

Father wanted to be the corpse at every funeral, the bride at every wedding, and the baby at every christening.

Alice Roosevelt Longworth (1884–1980), daughter of Theodore Roosevelt, twenty-sixth American president

We are all worms, but I do believe that I am a glow-worm.

Sir Winston Churchill (1874–1965), English prime minister and author

How glorious it is—and also how painful—to be an exception.

Alfred de Musset (1810–1857), French poet

A man who is eating or lying with his wife or preparing to go to sleep in humility, thankfulness and temperance, is, by Christian standards, in an infinitely *higher* state than one who is listening to Bach or reading Plato in a state of pride.

C. S. Lewis (1898–1963), English novelist

HAIR
TONIC
envy

Sin: Envy

Definition: (eńvē), *n.* a feeling of discontent or jealousy, usually with ill will at seeing another's superiority, advantages, or success. 2. desire for some advantage possessed by another.

See: ambition; pique; jealousy; rivalry; spite; paranoia; suspicion; wariness; reproach; acrimony; virulence; petulance; watchfulness; bitterness; indignation; rivalry; contentiousness; spleen; rancor; alienation; disaffection; estrangement; animosity; bitterness; enmity; hostility; mistrust; affront; discontent; frustration; peevishness; sourness; malice; suspicion; wariness; leeriness; apprehension; invidiousness; prejudice; desire; hunger; resentment; mistrust; protest; distrust; vindictiveness; displeasure

See also: begrudge; crave; long; thirst; yearn; want; fancy; malign; oppose; chase; emulate; pursue; grouse; whine; pine; languish; favor; prefer; lust after; hanker after; have ill will; wish in vain; eat one's heart out; take offense; cry for the moon; gasp for; itch for; set one's cap for; burn for; die for; raven for; have hard feelings; dote on; object to; die over; turn green; have a jaundiced eye; be vexed; be hostile; be resistant; be a bad sport; be back-biting; be disgruntled; be ill-disposed; be teed off; be hacked off; be ticked off; be pissed off; be cross; be a green-eyed monster; be crabby; be sulky; be pouty; be grouchy; be stung; be galled; be miffed; be sore; be unsated; be yellow-eyed; be annoyed

Envy hit him . . . like lack of oxygen.

William McIlvanney (b. 1936), English novelist

Meeting with John Kennedy's aide Ted Sorenson shortly after Kennedy's inaugural address, Richard Nixon remarked that there were things in the speech he would liked to have said. "Do you mean the part about 'Ask not what your country can do for you . . .?' said Sorenson. "No," replied Nixon, "the part beginning 'I do solemnly swear . . .'"

As recounted by Clifton Fadiman (b. 1904), American author and editor

Frankly, I don't mind not being president, I just mind that someone else is.

Edward M. Kennedy (b. 1932), American politician

Beggars do not envy millionaires, though of course they will envy other beggars who are more successful.

Bertrand Russell (1872–1970), English philosopher

Man will do many things to get himself loved, he will do all things to get himself envied.

Mark Twain (1835–1910), American humorist

Jealousy is all the fun you *think* they had.

Erica Jong (b. 1942), American poet and novelist

Go back to that wonderful Alan Jay Lerner song in *Camelot*, the one about "I wonder what the king is doing tonight." We really want to know what the king is up to. It must be something bred into us from peasantry.

Liz Smith (b. 1923), American gossip columnist

Her eyes are all awry, her teeth are foul with mould; green poisonous gall overflows her breast, venom drips from her tongue. She never smiles, save at the sight of another's troubles: she never sleeps, disturbed with wakeful cares; unwelcome to her is the sight of men's success, and with the sight she pines away: she gnaws and is gnawed, herself her own punishment.

Ovid (43 B.C.–A.D. 17), Roman poet, on envy

Malice may be sometimes out of breath, but never envy.

George, Lord Halifax (1881–1959), English statesman

Were there none who were discontented with what they have, the world would never reach anything better.

Florence Nightingale (1820–1910), English nurse and hospital reformer

I am sure the grapes are sour.

Aesop (sixth century B.C.), supposed author of Greek fables

Men can endure the praise of others so long as they believe that the actions praised are within their own power; they envy whatever they consider to be beyond it.

Thucydides (471?–400? B.C.), Greek historian

[Envy is] the most corroding of the vices, and also the greatest power in any land.

J. M. Barrie (1860–1937), Scottish novelist and playwright

We spend our time envying people whom we wouldn't wish to be.

Jean Rostand (1894–1977), French biologist and man of letters

[There is] far less envy in America than in France, and far less wit.

Stendhal (1783–1842), French novelist

Whenever a friend succeeds a little something in me dies.

Gore Vidal (b. 1925), American novelist, playwright, and essayist

For one man who sincerely pities our misfortunes, there are a thousand who sincerely hate our success.

Charles Caleb Colton (1780–1832), English Anglican clergyman

Success: *n.* The one unpardonable sin against one's fellows.

Ambrose Bierce (1842–1914), American writer

Our nature holds so much envy and malice that our pleasure in our own advantages is not so great as our distress at others'.

Plutarch (46?–120?), Greek biographer

The happiness of others is never bearable for long.

Françoise Sagan (b. 1935), French novelist

Moral indignation is in most cases 2 percent moral, 48 percent indignation, and 50 percent envy.

Vittorio DeSica (1901–1974), Italian actor and film director

In a consumer society there are inevitably two kinds of slaves: the prisoners of addiction and the prisoners of envy.

Ivan Illich (b. 1926), Austrian-born American theologian and author

Fools may our scorn, not envy, raise.
For envy is a kind of praise.

John Gay (1685–1732), English poet and playwright

Envy among other ingredients has a mixture of the love of justice in it. We are more angry at undeserved than at deserved good-fortune.

William Hazlitt (1778–1830), English essayist and critic

The man with a toothache thinks everyone happy whose teeth are sound.
George Bernard Shaw (1856–1950), Irish playwright, author, and critic

Never having been able to succeed in the world, he took his revenge by speaking ill of it.
Voltaire (1694–1778), French author

Spite is never lonely; envy always tags along.
Mignon McLaughlin (b. 1930), American writer

While the noble man lives in trust and openness with himself . . . the man of *ressentiment* is neither upright nor naive nor honest and straightforward with himself. His soul squints: his spirit loves hiding places, secret paths and back doors, everything covert strikes him as his world, his security, his refreshment; he understands how to keep silent, how not to forget, how to wait, how to be provisionally self-deprecating and humble.
Friedrich Nietzsche (1844–1900), German philosopher and poet

Jealousy is the most dreadfully involuntary of all sins.
Iris Murdoch (b. 1919), Irish-born English novelist

The envied are like bureaucrats; the more impersonal they are, the greater the illusion (for themselves and for others) of their power.
John Berger (b. 1926), English art critic and writer

That, of course, is why Envy is so unenviable a dominating emotion. All the seven deadly sins are self-destroying, morbid appetites, but in their early stages at least lust and gluttony, avarice and sloth know some gratification, while anger and pride have power, even though that power eventually destroys itself. Envy is impotent, numbed with fear, yet never ceasing in its appetite; and it knows no gratification save endless self-torment. It has the ugliness of a trapped rat that has gnawed its own foot in its effort to escape.
Angus Wilson (1913–1991), English writer and biographer

I am the kind of writer that people think other people are reading.
V. S. Naipul (b. 1932), West Indian novelist and essayist

In Pope I cannot read a line,
but with a sigh I wish it mine.
Jonathan Swift (1667–1745), Anglo-Irish author

War and Peace maddens me because I didn't write it myself, and worse, I couldn't.
Jeffrey Archer (b. 1940), English author

Authors are like cattle going to a fair: Those of the same field can never move on without butting one another.
Walter Savage Landor (1775–1864), English author

As there are none more ambitious of fame than those who are conversant in poetry, it is very natural for such as have not succeeded in it to depreciate the works of those who have.
Joseph Addison (1672–1719), English essayist

The praise of ancient authors proceeds not from the reverence of the dead, but from the competition and mutual envy of the living.
Thomas Hobbes (1588–1679), English philosopher

What poet would not grieve to see
His brother write as well as he?
But rather than they should excel,
Would wish his rivals all in Hell?
Jonathan Swift (1667–1745), Anglo-Irish author

The literary world is made of up little confederacies, each looking upon its own members as the lights of the universe; and considering all others as mere transient meteors, doomed to fall and be forgotten, while its own luminaries are to shine steadily on to immortality.
Washington Irving (1783–1859), American author

The only reward to be expected from the cultivation of literature is contempt if one fails and hatred if one succeeds.
Voltaire (1694–1778), French author

Envy's memory is nothing but a row of hooks to hang up grudges on.
John Watson Foster (1836–1917), American statesman

If envy, like anger, did not burn itself in its own fire, and consume and destroy those persons it possesses before it can destroy those it wishes worst to, it would set the whole world on fire, and leave the most excellent persons the most miserable.
Edward Hyde (1609–1674), English statesman and historian

The envious die not once, but as oft as the envied win applause.
Baltasar Gracian (1601–1658), Spanish writer and Jesuit priest

Wherever I find envy, I take a pleasure in provoking it; I always praise before an envious man those who make him grow pale.
Montesquieu (1689–1755), French lawyer, writer, and philosopher

If we did but know how little some enjoy of the great things that they possess, there would not be much envy in the world.
Edward Young (1683–1765), English poet

One of envy's favourite stratagems is the attempt to provoke envy in the envied one.
Leslie Farber (1912–1981), American psychoanalyst

Jealousy sees things always with magnifying glasses which make little things large, of dwarfs giants, of suspicions truths.
Miguel de Cervantes (1547–1616), Spanish novelist

All jealousy must be strangled in its birth, or time will soon make it strong enough to overcome the truth.
Sir William D'Avenant (1606–1668), English poet and playwright

What a miserable thing life is: You're living in clover, only the clover isn't good enough.
Bertolt Brecht (1898–1956), German poet and playwright

It is not irritating to be where one is. It is only irritating to think one would like to be somewhere else.
John Cage (1912–1992), American composer

To have a grievance is to have a purpose in life.
Eric Hoffer (1902–1983), American author

Jealousy is like a bad toothache. It does not let a person do anything, not even sit still. It can only be walked off.
Milan Kundera (b. 1929), Czech author

If envy were a fever, all the world would be ill.
Danish proverb

Envy is a littleness of soul, which cannot see beyond a certain point, and if it does not occupy the whole space feels itself excluded.
William Hazlitt (1778–1830), English essayist and critic

Our envy always lasts much longer than the happiness of those we envy.

1680), French author

Even success softens not the heart of the envious.
Pindar (518–438 B.C.), Greek lyric poet

Deformed persons and eunuchs, and old men and bastards, are envious, for he that cannot possibly mend his own case, will do what he can to impair another's.
Francis Bacon (1561–1626), English philosopher and author

Envy and hatred are always united. They gather strength from each other by being engaged upon the same object.
Jean de La Bruyere (1645–1696), French essayist

Envy is the most stupid of vices, for there is no single advantage to be gained from it.
Honoré de Balzac (1799–1850), French novelist

We are not satisfied to be right, unless we can prove others to be quite wrong.
William Hazlitt (1778–1830), English essayist and critic

Envy which talks and cries out is always maladroit; it is the envy which keeps silent that one ought to fear.
Antoine de Rivarol (1753–1801), French satirist

What makes us discontented with our condition is the absurdly exaggerated idea we have of the happiness of others.
Anonymous

Envy honours the dead in order to insult the living.
Helvétius (1715–1771), French philosopher

It is not given to everyone to find the right outlet for his envy.
Jean Rostand (1894–1977), French biologist and man of letters

Whereas true admiration keeps its distance, respecting the discrepancy between the admirer and the admired one, envy's assault upon its object with a barrage of compliments serves not only its need to assert itself in the costume of admiration, but also the lust of the envier to possess the very quality that initially incited his envy.
Leslie Farber (1912–1981), American psychoanalyst

Potter bears a grudge against potter, and craftsman against craftsman, and beggar is envious of beggar, the bard of bard.
Hesiod (eighth century B.C.), Greek poet

The player envies only the player, the poet envies only the poet.
William Hazlitt (1778–1830), English essayist and critic

The gilded sheath of pity conceals the dagger of envy.
Friedrich Nietzsche (1844–1900), German philosopher and poet

Envy is as persistent as memory, as intractable as a head cold.
Harry Stein (b. 1948), American journalist

Envy and wrath shorten the life.
The Apocrypha, Ecclesiasticus 30:24

People may go on talking forever of the jealousies of pretty women; but for real genuine, hard-working envy, there is nothing like an ugly woman with a taste for admiration.
Emily Eden (1797–1869), English-born Indian novelist

The secret of my success is that no woman has ever been jealous of me.
Elsa Maxwell (1883–1963), American gossip columnist

[Jealousy is] the green sickness.
William Shakespeare (1564–1616), English playwright and poet

Believe all the good you can of everyone. Do not measure others by yourself. If they have advantages which you have not, let your liberality keep pace with their good fortune. Envy no one, and you need envy no one.
William Hazlitt (1778–1830), English essayist and critic

Do not measure another's coat on your own body.
Malay proverb

Grudge not another what you cannot attain yourself.
English proverb

The greatest of all secrets is knowing how to reduce the force of envy.
Cardinal de Retz (1613–1679), French clergyman and politician

Trust to me, ladies, and do not envy a splendor which does not constitute happiness.
Josephine de Beauharnais (1763–1814), first wife of Napoleon

Love and envy make a man pine, which other affections do not, because they are not continual.
Francis Bacon (1561–1626), English philosopher and author

The dullard's envy of brilliant men is always assuaged by the suspicion that they will come to a bad end.
Max Beerbohm (1872–1956), English critic and caricaturist

A man is very apt to complain of the ingratitude of those who have risen far above him.
Samuel Johnson (1709–1784), English author

People hate those who make them feel their own inferiority.
Lord Chesterfield (1694–1773), English statesman

Arrogance in a person of merit affronts us more than arrogance in those without merit: Merit itself is an affront.
Friedrich Nietzsche (1844–1900), German philosopher and poet

Confronted by outstanding merit in another, there is no way of saving one's ego except by love.
Johann Wolfgang von Goethe (1749–1832), German poet and philosopher

We grow tired of everything but turning others into ridicule, and congratulating ourselves on their defects.
William Hazlitt (1778–1830), English essayist and critic

Passions tyrannize over mankind; but ambition keeps all the others in check.
Jean de La Bruyere (1645–1696), French essayist

Ambition is pitiless. Any merit that it cannot use it finds despicable.
Joseph Joubert (1754–1824), French moralist

Nothing is enough to the man for whom enough is too little.
Epicurus (341–270 B.C.), Greek philosopher

Everybody wants to *be* somebody: nobody wants to *grow*.
Johann Wolfgang von Goethe (1749–1832), German poet and philosopher

Those who are contemptuous of everyone are more than anyone terrified of contempt.
Logan Pearsall Smith (1865–1946), American essayist

A man that is busy and inquisitive is commonly envious. For envy is a gadding passion, and walketh the streets, and doth not keep at home.
Francis Bacon (1561–1626), English philosopher and author

As iron is eaten by rust, so are the envious consumed by envy.
Livy (59 B.C.–A.D. 17), Roman historian

Envy, like the worm, never runs but to the fairest fruit; like a cunning bloodhound, it singles out the fattest deer in the flock.
Francis Beaumont (1584–1616), English playwright

Felt a twinge of jealousy, green as a worm, wriggling deep in my center.
W.P. Kinsella (b. 1935), Canadian writer

It [jealousy] was like a taste in his mouth.
Joyce Carol Oates (b. 1938), American author

A man who shows me his wealth is like a beggar who shows me his poverty; they are both looking for alms . . . the rich for the alms of envy, the poor for the alms of my pity.
Ben Hecht (1894–1964), American author

He that envies is possessed of self-made hurts.
Shaikh Saadi (1184?–1291), Persian poet

[Envy is] the beginning of hell in this life, and a passion not to be excused.
Robert Burton (1577–1640), English clergyman and author

There is but one man who can believe himself free from envy, and it is he who has never examined his own heart.
Helvétius (1715–1771), French philosopher

There is not a passion so strongly rooted in the human heart as envy.
Richard Brinsley Sheridan (1751–1816), Irish-born English playwright

Envy is a coal come hissing from hell.
Philip James Bailey (1816–1902), English poet

Jealousy is said to be the offspring of love. Yet unless the parent makes haste to strangle the child, the child will not rest till it has poisoned the parent.
Julius Hare (1795–1855), English Anglican clergyman

When you cannot get a thing, then is the time to have contempt for it.
Baltasar Gracian (1601–1658), Spanish prose writer and Jesuit priest

Since we cannot attain to greatness, let us revenge ourselves by railing at it.
Michel Eyquem de Montaigne (1533–1592), French essayist

Few men have the strength of character to rejoice in a friend's success without a touch of envy.
Aeschylus (525–456 B.C.), Greek tragic playwright

The worst part of success is to try finding someone who is happy for you.
Bette Midler (b. 1945), comedian, actor, and singer

The envious man grows lean at the success of his neighbor.
Horace (65–8 B.C.), Roman lyric poet and satirist

Whoever feels pain in hearing a good character of his neighbor, will feel a pleasure in the reverse. And those who despair to rise in distinction by their virtues, are happy if others can be depressed to a level with themselves.
Benjamin Franklin (1706–1790), American statesman, scientist, and author

Envy with a pale and meager face (whose body was so lean that one might tell all her bones, and whose garment was so tatter'd that it was easy to number every thread) stood shooting at stars, whose darts fell down again on her own face.
John Lyly (1554?–1606), English author

I am Envy, begotten of a chimneysweeper and an oysterwife. I cannot read, and therefore wish all books were burnt. I am lean with seeing others eat.
Christopher Marlowe (1564–1593), English playwright

The envious will die, but envy never.
Molière (1622–1673), French actor and playwright

Envy writhes; it does not laugh.
Lord Byron (1788–1824), English poet

Even in envy may be discerned something of an instinct of justice, something of a wish to see fair play, and things on a level.
Leigh Hunt (1784–1859), English author

Probably the greatest harm done by vast wealth is the harm that we of moderate means do ourselves when we let the vices of envy and hatred enter deep into our own nature.
Theodore Roosevelt (1858–1919), twenty-sixth American president

All fame is dangerous: good bringeth envy; bad, shame.
Thomas Fuller (1608–1661), English clergyman

The race of men is of a jealous temperament.
Homer (850?–800? B.C.), Greek epic poet

Jealousy is cruel as the grave; the coals thereof are coals of fire.
The Old Testament, Song of Solomon 8:6

[Envy] reigns more among bad poets than among any other set of men.
Joseph Addison (1672–1719), English writer

It seems to me we can never give up longing and wishing while we are thoroughly alive. There are certain things we feel to be beautiful and good, and we must hunger after them.
George Eliot (1819–1880), English novelist

Jealousy is a kind of civil war in the soul, where judgment and imagination are at perpetual jars.
William Penn (1644–1718), English Quaker and founder of Pennsylvania

He was a man of strong passions, and the green-eyed monster ran up his leg and bit him to the bone.
P. G. Wodehouse (1881–1975), English writer and humorist

It is not for man to rest in absolute contentment. He is born to hopes and aspirations as the sparks fly upward, unless he has brutified his nature and quenched the spirit of immortality which is his portion.
Robert Southey (1774–1843), English poet

Every other sin hath some pleasure annexed to it, or will admit of some excuse, but envy wants both. We should strive against it, for if indulged in it will be to us a foretaste of hell on earth.
Richard Eugene Burton (1861–1940), American poet and professor

Envy is like a fly that passes all a body's sounder parts, and dwells upon the sores.
George Chapman (1559?–1634), English poet and playwright

Wrath killeth the foolish man, and envy slayeth the silly one.
The Old Testament, Job 5:2

If envy, like anger, did not burn itself in its own fire, and consume and destroy those persons it possesses before it can destroy those it wishes worst to, it would set the whole world on fire, and leave the most excellent persons the most miserable.
Edward Hyde (1609–1674), English statesman and historian

Other passions have objects to flatter them, and which seem content and satisfy them for a while. There is power in ambition, pleasure in luxury, and pelf in covetousness; but envy can gain nothing but vexation.
Michel Eyquem de Montaigne (1533–1592), French essayist

Expect not praise without envy until you are dead. Honors bestowed on the illustrious dead have in them no admixture of envy; for the living pity the dead; and pity and envy, like oil and vinegar, assimilate not.
Charles Caleb Colton (1780–1832), English Anglican clergyman

As a moth gnaws a garment, so doth envy consume a man.
John Chrysostom (345?–407), father of the Greek church

Nothing is more humiliating than to see idiots succeed in enterprises we have failed in.
Gustave Flaubert (1821–1880), French novelist

Nothing arouses ambition so much in the heart as the trumpet-clang of another's fame.
Baltasar Gracian (1601–1658), Spanish writer and Jesuit priest

Jealousy is like a polished glass held to the lips when life is in doubt; if there be breath, it will catch the damp and show it.
John Dryden (1631–1700), English poet

He is a man of sense who does not grieve for what he has not, but rejoices in what he has.
Epictetus (55?–135?), Greek stoic philosopher in Rome

Men . . . always think that something they are going to get is better than what they have got.
John Oliver Hobbes (1867–1906), American-born English novelist and playwright

Take full account of the excellencies which you possess, and in gratitude remember how you would hanker after them, if you had them not.
Marcus Aurelius (121–180), Roman emperor and philosopher

Long only for what you have.
André Gide (1869–1951), French author and critic

If there is a sin against life, it consists perhaps not so much in despairing of life as in hoping for another, and in eluding the implacable grandeur of this life.
Albert Camus (1913–1960), French existentialist author

What you really value is what you miss, not what you have.
Jorge Luis Borges (1899–1986), Argentine writer

We always have enough to be happy if we are enjoying what we do have—and not worrying about what we don't have.
Ken Keyes, Jr. (1921–1995), American writer

There is a mortal breed most full of futility. In contempt of what is at hand, they strain into the future, hunting impossibilities on the wings of ineffectual hopes.
Pindar (518?–438 B.C.), Greek lyric poet

A man can refrain from wanting what he has not, and cheerfully make the best of a bird in the hand.
Marcus Annaeus Seneca (3 B.C.?–A.D. 65?), Roman statesman and philosopher

Jealousy, he thought, was as physical as fear; the same dryness of the mouth, the thudding heart, the restlessness which destroyed appetite and peace.
P. D. James (b. 1920), English novelist

The superiority of the distant over the present is only due to the mass and variety of the pleasures that can be suggested, compared with the poverty of those that can at any time be felt.
George Santayana (1863–1952), Spanish-born American poet and philosopher

Mankind, by the perverse depravity of their nature, esteem that which they have most desired as of no value the moment it is possessed, and torment themselves with fruitless wishes for that which is beyond their reach.
François de Salignac de la Mothe-Fénelon (1651–1715), French Roman Catholic theologian

Do not spoil what you have by desiring what you have not; remember that what you now have was once among the things only hoped for.
Epicurus (341–270 B.C.), Greek philosopher

We spend our time searching for security and hate it when we get it.
John Steinbeck (1902–1968), American novelist

Is there no end to this escalation of desire?
Marya Mannes (1904–1990), American writer

What you can't get is just what suits you.
French proverb

Her jealousy never slept.
Mary Shelley (1797–1851), English novelist

We love in others what we lack ourselves, and would be everything but what we are.
R. H. Stoddard (1825–1903), American poet and literary critic

When you don't have any money, the problem is food. When you have money, it's sex. When you have both, it's health. If everything is simply jake, then you're frightened of death.
J. P. Donleavy (b. 1926), Irish-born American novelist

Diogenes was asked what wine he liked best, and he answered, "Somebody else's."
Michel Eyquem de Montaigne (1533–1592), French essayist

We always long for forbidden things, and desire what is denied us.
François Rabelais (1490–1553), French humorist and satirist

Man's heart is never satisfied; the snake would swallow the elephant.
Chinese proverb

When every blessed thing you have is made of silver, or of gold, you long for simple pewter.
W. S. Gilbert (1836–1911), English librettist

I'd rather have written *Cheers* than anything I've written.
Kurt Vonnegut (b. 1922), American novelist

Jealousy that surrounds me like a too-warm room.
William H. Gass (b. 1924), American author and philosopher

Man would be otherwise. That is the essence of the specifically human.
Antonio Machado (1875–1939), Spanish poet

We are under the spell always of what is distant from us. It is not in our nature to desire passionately what is near at hand.
Alec Waugh (1898–1981), English novelist

In all climates, under all skies, man's happiness is always somewhere else.
Giacomo Leopardi (1798–1837), Italian poet

Life is a hospital in which every patient is possessed by the desire of changing his bed. One would prefer to suffer near the fire, and another is certain he would get well if he were by the window.
Charles Baudelaire (1821–1867), French poet

There are three wants which can never be satisfied: that of the rich, who want something more; that of the sick, who want something different; and that of the traveler, who says, "Anywhere but here."
Ralph Waldo Emerson (1803–1882), American essayist and poet

Jealousy is never satisfied with anything short of an omniscience that would detect the subtlest fold of the heart.
George Eliot (1819–1880), English novelist

Men would be angels, angels would be gods.
Alexander Pope (1688–1744), English poet

I want to be able to live without a crowded calendar. I want to be able to read a book without feeling guilty, or go to a concert when I like.
Golda Meir (1898–1978), Israeli prime minister

Oh God, don't envy me, I have my own pains.
Barbra Streisand (b. 1942), American singer, actor, and director

I'd like to be a truck driver. I think you could run your life that way. It wouldn't be such a bad way of doing it. It would offer a chance to be alone.
Princess Anne (b. 1920), daughter of Queen Elizabeth II of England

I just want to be an ordinary girl.
Princess Stephanie (b. 1965), daughter of Princess Grace and Prince Ranier of Monaco

Pray the gods do not envy your happiness!
Euripides (480?–406? B.C.), Greek tragic playwright

Envy is an insult to oneself.
Yevgeny Yevtushenko (b. 1933), Russian poet

Instead of comparing our lot with that of those who are more fortunate than we are, we should compare it with the lot of the great majority of our fellow men. It then appears that we are among the privileged.
Helen Keller (1880–1968), American writer and lecturer

There is a sort of jealousy which needs very little fire; it is hardly a passion, but a blight bred in the cloudy, damp despondency of uneasy egoism.
George Eliot (1819–1880), English novelist

If we only wanted to be happy it would be easy; but we want to be happier than other people, which is almost always difficult, since we think them happier than they are.
Montesquieu (1689–1755), French lawyer, writer, and philosopher

No story ever looks as bad as the story you've just bought; no story ever looks as good as the story the other fellow just bought.
Irving Thalberg (1899–1936), American film executive

If envy would burn, there would be no use of wood.
Yugoslav proverb

Everyone expects to go further than his father went; everyone expects to be better than he was born and every generation has one big impulse in its heart—to exceed all the other generations of the past in all the things that make life worth living.
William Allen White (1868–1944), American editor and writer

The sieve with a thousand holes finds fault with the basket.
Indian proverb

Compete, don't envy.
Arab proverb

I am convinced that we have a degree of delight, and that no small one, in the real misfortunes and pains of others.
Edmund Burke (1729–1797), Irish-born English statesman, orator, and philosopher

One likes people much better when they're battered down by a prodigious siege of misfortune than when they triumph.
Virginia Woolf (1882–1941), English author

Man loves malice, but not against one-eyed men nor the unfortunate, but against the fortunate and proud.
Martial (40?–104?), Spanish-born Latin epigrammatist

If there were in the world today any large number of people who desired their own happiness more than they desired the unhappiness of others, we could have a paradise in a few years.

Bertrand Russell (1872–1970), English philosopher

If all the fornicators and adulterers in England were hanged by the neck till they be dead, John Bunyan, the object of their envy, would be still alive and well.

John Bunyan (1628–1688), English preacher and author

Malice sucks up the greater part of its own venom, and poisons itself. Vice leaves, like an ulcer in the flesh, repentance in the soul, which is always scratching and bloodying itself; for reason overcomes all other griefs and sorrows, but it begets repentance.

Michel Eyquem de Montaigne (1533–1592), French essayist

[Jealousy is. . .] The vulture who explores our innermost liver, and drags out our heart and nerves.

Petronius (first century A.D.), probable author of the *Satyricon*

The greatest harm that you can do unto the envious, is to do well.

John Lyly (1554?–1606), English author

Wrath is cruel, and anger is outrageous, but who is able to stand before envy?

The Old Testament, Proverbs 27:4

Envy is mere unmixed and genuine evil; it pursues a hateful end by despicable means and desires not so much its own happiness as another's misery.

Samuel Johnson (1709–1784), English author

There is such malice in men as to rejoice in misfortunes and from another's woes to draw delight.

Terence (190–159 B.C.), Roman poet

Envy eats nothing but its own heart.
German proverb

Jealousy . . . descended on his spirit like a choking and pestilence-laden cloud.
Thomas Wolfe (1900–1938), American novelist

Other people's eggs have two yolks.
Bulgarian proverb

It is a sickening thing to think how many angry and evil passions the mere name of admitted excellence brings into full activity.
Sir Walter Scott (1771–1832), Scottish poet and novelist

There is nothing so irritating as somebody with less intelligence and more sense than we have.
Don Herold (nineteenth–twentieth century), American author

Love looks through a telescope; envy, through a microscope.
Josh Billings (1818–1885), American humorist

I believe in luck: How else can you explain the success of those you don't like?
Jean Cocteau (1889–1963), French poet, novelist, and director

Envy honours the dead in order to insult the living.
Helvétius (1715–1771), French philosopher

Whereas true admiration keeps its distance, respecting the discrepancy between the admirer and the admired one, envy's assault upon its object with a barrage of compliments serves not only its need to assert itself in the costume of admiration, but also the lust of the envier to possess the very quality that initially incited his envy.
Leslie Farber (1912–1981), American psychoanalyst

Each [of my wives] was jealous and resentful of my preoccupation with business. Yet none showed any visible aversion to sharing the proceeds.
J. Paul Getty (1892–1976), American oil magnate

What frenzy dictates, jealousness believes.
John Gay (1685–1732), English poet and playwright

When we cannot get what we love, we must love what is within our reach.
French proverb

[Jealousy is] uneasiness of the mind, caused by the consideration of a good we desire, obtained by one we think should not have it before us.
John Locke (1632–1704), English philosopher

A prudent man will think more important what fate has conceded to him, than what it has denied.
Baltasar Gracian (1601–1658), Spanish writer and Jesuit priest

Man is the only creature that strives to surpass himself, and yearns for the impossible.
Eric Hoffer (1902–1983), American author

Sometimes we owe a friend to the lucky circumstance that we give him no cause for envy.
Friedrich Nietzsche (1844–1900), German philosopher and poet

It is not given to the children of men to be philosophers without envy. Lookers-on can hardly bear the spectacle of the great world.
Walter Bagehot (1826–1877), English economist

Envy is capable of serving the valuable social function of making the rich moderate their habits for fear of arousing it.
Sir Keith Joseph (1918–1994), English Conservative politician

The best condition in life is not to be so rich as to be envied nor so poor as to be damned.
Josh Billings (1818–1885), American humorist

Helpless, unknown, and unremembered, most human beings, however sensitive, idealistic, intelligent, go through life as passengers rather than chauffeurs. Although we may pretend that it is the chauffeur who is the social inferior . . . most of us, like Toad of Toad Hall, would not mind a turn at the wheel ourselves.
Ralph Harper (b. 1915), American clergyman and author

Some folks rail against other folks, because other folks have what some folks would be glad of.
Henry Fielding (1707–1754), English novelist and playwright

Glamour cannot exist without personal social envy being a common and widespread emotion.
John Berger (b. 1926), English writer

The heart of the jealous knows the best and most satisfying love, that of the other's bed, where the rival perfects the lover's imperfections.
Djuna Barnes (1892–1982), American author and poet

Ambition is a Dead Sea fruit, and the greatest peril to the soul is that one is likely to get precisely what he is seeking.
Edward Dahlberg (1909–1977), American author and critic

Man is fond of counting his troubles, but he does not count his joys. If he counted them up as he ought to, he would see that every lot has enough happiness provided for it.

Fyodor Dostoevski (1821–1881), Russian novelist

There are just two creatures I would envy—a horse in his wild state traversing the forests of Asia, or an oyster on some of the deserted shores of Europe.

Robert Burns (1759–1796), Scottish poet

He who is not envied is not enviable.

Aeschylus (525?–456 B.C.), Greek playwright

Comparisons of one's lot with others' teaches us nothing and enfeebles the will.

Thornton Wilder (1897–1975), American novelist and playwright

Envy has no other quality but that of detracting virtue.

Livy (59 B.C.–A.D. 17), Roman historian

If one has one cow, it is always better not to be too familiar with those who have seven.

Phyllis Bottome (1884–1963), English-born American writer

She wished all the faculties she did not share to be looked on as diseases.

Madame de Stäel (1766–1817), French writer

Jealousy is said to be the offspring of love. Yet unless the parent makes haste to strangle the child, the child will not rest until; it has poisoned the parent.

J. C. Hare (1795–1855), English Anglican clergyman

All the tyrants of Sicily never invented a worse torment than envy.

Horace (65–8 B.C.), Roman lyric poet and satirist

Unlike true admiration, which, because it is free of conscious will always has the option of silence, envy's imitation of admiration clamours for public acknowledgement; the more stinging the envy, the more ardently must the envious one dramatize himself as an admirer whose passion overshadows and shames the more reticent responses of others.

Leslie Farber (1912–1981), American psychoanalyst

Envy is a pain of mind that successful men cause their neighbors.

Onasander (first century B.C.–first century A.D.), Greek philosopher

In few men is it part of nature to respect a friend's prosperity without begrudging him.

Aeschylus (525–456 B.C.), Greek tragic playwright

He that cannot possibly mend his own case will do what he can to impair another's.

Francis Bacon (1561–1626), English philosopher and author

Those who speak against the great do not usually speak from morality, but from envy.

Walter Savage Landor (1775–1864), English author

Even success softens not the heart of the envious.

Pindar (518–438 B.C.), Greek lyric poet

Our nature holds so much envy and malice that our pleasure in our own advantages is not so great as our distress at others'.

Plutarch (46?–120?), Greek biographer

We are often vain of even the most criminal of our passions; but envy is so shameful a passion that we never dare to acknowledge it.

Duc François de la Rochefoucauld (1613–1680), French author

anger
TNT

anger

Sin: Anger

Definition: (anǵ-ər), *n.* a strong feeling of displeasure and belligerence aroused by a real or supposed wrong

See: wrath; excitation; animosity; vengeance; irritability; disapprobation; fury; huffiness; ill humor; petulance; acrimony; hatred; hostility; frenzy; exasperation; rage; indignity; bitterness; enmity; malice; antagonism; belligerence; irascibility; temper; aggravation; contempt; displeasure; asperity; bad blood; acrimony; ill will; resentment; detestation; loathing; abhorrence; impatience; disaffection; estrangement; alienation; dissension; repugnance; antipathy; aversion; revulsion; agitation; high dudgeon; malediction; grumpiness; irateness; pique

See also: affront; bait; gall; incense; madden; rankle; seethe; vex; bristle; enrage; rant; annoy; insult; goad; stew; arouse; ruffle; spite; outrage; peeve; embroil; gnaw; incense; infuriate; envenom; bug; bother; needle; fume; explode; ferment; rampage; shout; glare; glower; growl; scowl; upset; frown; snarl; bark; bite; snap; blow up; steam up; stir up; take offense; take umbrage; see red; go berserk; fan the flame; add fuel to the fire; raise one's hackles; get on one's nerves; get under one's skin; get one's goat; get up one's nose; get one's dander up; push too far; bead one's fangs; stir the blood; set at loggerheads; have a conniption; be livid; be cross; be apoplectic; be miffed; be furious; be disgruntled

If I die, I forgive you; if I recover, we shall see.
Spanish Proverb

Many people lose their tempers merely from seeing you keep yours.
Frank Moore Colby (1865–1925), American editor

Anger is electric, exhilarating. The angry person knows without a doubt he is alive. And the state of unaliveness, or partial aliveness, is so frequent and so frightening, the condition of inertia common, almost, as dirt, that there's no wonder anger feels like treasure. It goes through the body like a jet of freezing water; it fills the veins with purpose; it alerts the lazy eye and ear; the sluggish limbs cry out for movement; the torpid lungs grow rich with easy breath. Anger flows through our entire body, stem to stern. . . .
Mary Gordon (b. 1949), American author

I never work better than when I am inspired by anger; for when I am angry, I can write, pray, and preach well, for then my whole temperament is quickened, my understanding sharpened, and all mundane vexations and temptations depart.
Martin Luther (1483–1546), German religious reformer

Anger is an expensive luxury in which men of only a certain income can indulge.
George William Curtis (1824–1892), American author and editor

Every normal man must be tempted at times to spit on his hands, hoist the black flag, and begin slitting throats.
H. L. Mencken (1880–1956), American satirist and editor

He spoke with a certain what-is-it in his voice, and I could see that, if not actually disgruntled, he was far from being gruntled.
P. G. Wodehouse (1881–1975), English writer and humorist

There is nothing more galling to angry people than the coolness of those on whom they wish to vent their spleen.
Alexandre Dumas (1802–1870), French novelist and playwright

Impotent hatred is the most horrible of all emotions; one should hate nobody whom one cannot destroy.
Johann Wolfgang von Goethe (1749–1832), German poet and philosopher

One should not lose one's temper unless one is certain of getting more and more angry to the end.
William Butler Yeats (1865–1939), Irish poet and playwright

When angry, count ten, before you speak; if very angry, an hundred.
Thomas Jefferson (1743–1826), third American president

When angry, count four; when very angry, swear.
Mark Twain (1835–1910), American writer

Men are very queer animals—a mixture of horse-nervousness, ass-stubbornness, and camel-malice.
T. H. Huxley (1825–1895), English biologist and educator

Most men's anger about religion is as if two men should quarrel for a lady neither of them care for.
Lord Halifax (1881–1959), English statesman

Violence suits those who have nothing to lose.
Jean-Paul Sartre (1905–1980), French existentialist author

The first step in claiming yourself is anger.
Jamaica Kincaid (b. 1949), West Indies–born American writer

I was so mad you could have boiled a pot of water on my head.
Alice Childress (1917–1994), American novelist and playwright

Beware the fury of a patient man.
John Dryden (1631–1700), English poet

They buried the hatchet, but in a shallow, well-marked grave.
Dorothy Walworth (1900–1953), American novelist

There's no point in burying a hatchet if you're going to put up a marker on the site.
Sydney Harris (b. 1917), English-born American newspaper columnist

When my enemies stop hissing, I shall know I'm slipping.
Maria Callas (1923–1977), Greek-born American opera singer

Ethel Barrymore was exact in manners and expected from others the same courtesy. When she invited a young actress to dinner, her guest not only failed to appear but did not even bother to account for her absence. Several days later, the two women met unexpectedly at New York's Gallery of Modern Art. Lamely, the young woman began, "I think I was invited to your house for dinner last Thursday night."
"Oh yes," replied Ethel. "Did you come?"
Ethel Barrymore (1879–1959), American actor

Never forget what a man says to you when he is angry.
Henry Ward Beecher (1813–1887), American congregational clergyman

I have a right to my anger, and I don't want anybody telling me I shouldn't be, that it's not nice to be, and that something's wrong with me because I get angry.
Maxine Waters (b. 1938?), American politician

Anger as soon as fed is dead—
'Tis starving makes it fat.
Emily Dickinson (1830–1886), American poet

People in a temper often say a lot of silly, terrible things they mean.
Penelope Gilliatt (b. 1932), English novelist

To obtain another man's opinion of you, make him angry.
Oliver Wendell Holmes (1841–1935), American jurist

Hate seemed to crackle out of him in little flashes, like electricity in a cat's fur.
M. F. K. Fisher (1908–1992), American writer

My specialty is detached malevolence.
Alice Roosevelt Longworth (1884–1980), American author and socialite

I don't hate anyone. I dislike. But my dislike is equivalent of anyone else's hate.
Elsa Maxwell (1883–1963), American gossip columnist

Anger is a brief lunacy.
Horace (65–8 B.C.), Roman lyric poet and satirist

We boil at different degrees.
Ralph Waldo Emerson (1803–1882), American essayist and poet

There is a great deal of unmapped country within us which would have to be taken into account in an explanation of our gusts and storms.
George Eliot (1819–1880), English novelist

I have never known anyone worth a damn who wasn't irascible.
Ezra Pound (1885–1972), American poet

Anger is one of the sinews of the soul.
Thomas Fuller (1608–1661), English clergyman

Latent in every man is a venom of amazing bitterness, a black resentment; something that curses and loathes life, a feeling of being trapped, of having trusted and been fooled, of being the helpless prey of impotent rage, blind surrender, the victim of a savage ruthless power that gives and takes away, enlists a man, drops him, promises and betrays, and—crowning injury—inflicts on him the humiliation of feeling sorry for himself and of regarding this "power" as an intelligent, sentient being, capable of being touched.
Paul Valéry (1871–1945), French poet and philosopher

The man who gets angry at the right things and with the right people, and in the right way and at the right time and for the right length of time is commended.

Aristotle (384–322 B.C.), Greek philosopher

For thou shalt heap coals of fire upon his head, and the Lord shall reward thee.

The Old Testament, Proverbs 25:22

Malice is like a game of poker or tennis; you don't play it with anyone who is manifestly inferior to you.

Hilde Spiel (1911–1990), Austrian author

But hatred is a much more delightful passion and never cloys; It will make us all happy for the rest of our lives.

Lord Byron (1788–1824), English poet

It was hate at first sight, clean, pure, and strong as grain alcohol.

Elizabeth Peters (b. 1927), American novelist

I never hated a man enough to give him diamonds back.

Zsa Zsa Gabor (b. 1919), Hungarian-born American actor

The greatest hatred, like the greatest virtue and the worst dogs, is silent.

Jean Paul Richter (1763–1825), German novelist and humorist

You are done for—a living dead man—not when you stop loving but stop hating. Hatred preserves it: In it, in its chemistry, resides the "mystery" of life. Not for nothing is hatred still the best tonic ever discovered, for which any organism however feeble, has a tolerance.

E. M. Cioran (b. 1911), Rumanian-born French philosopher

You must embrace the man you hate, if you cannot be justified in knocking him down.

Lord Chesterfield (1694–1773), English statesman

If you fear making anyone mad, then you ultimately probe for the lowest common denominator of human achievement.

Jimmy Carter (b. 1924), thirty-ninth American president

The man of knowledge must be able not only to love his enemies but also to hate his friends.

Friedrich Nietzsche (1844–1900), German philosopher

Like all the sins except pride, anger is a perversion, caused by pride, of something in our nature which is innocent, necessary to our existence and good.

W. H. Auden (1907–1973), English poet

I know of no more disagreeable situation than to be left feeling generally angry without anybody in particular to be angry at.
Frank Moore Colby (1865–1925), American editor

Kindnesses are easily forgotten; but injuries?—what worthy man does not keep those in mind?
William Makepeace Thackeray (1811–1863), English author

The stupid neither forgive nor forget; the naïve forgive and forget; the wise forgive but do not forget.
Thomas Szasz (b. 1920), Hungarian-born American professor of psychiatry

Always remember, others may hate you. Those who hate you don't win unless you hate them. And then you destroy yourself.
Richard Nixon (1913–1994), thirty-seventh American president

Don't get mad. Get even.
John F. Kennedy (1917–1963), thirty-fifth American president

Men and women aren't really dogs: They only look like it and behave like it. Somewhere inside there is a great chagrin and a gnawing discontent.
D. H. Lawrence (1885–1930), English novelist

Bigotry may be roughly defined as the anger of men who have no opinions.
G. K. Chesterton (1874–1936), English journalist and author

Eat a third, drink a third, and leave a third of your stomach empty; then, should anger seize you, there will be room for its rage.
The Talmud

Anger always thinks it has power beyond its power.
Publilius Syrus (first century B.C.), Roman poet and actor

While love ceaselessly strives toward that which lies at the hiddenmost center, hatred only perceives the topmost surface and perceives it so exclusively that the devil of hatred, despite all his terror-inspiring cruelty, never is entirely free of ridicule and of a somewhat dilettantish aspect. One who hates is a man holding a magnifying-glass, and when he hates someone, he knows precisely that person's surface, from the soles of his feet all the way up to each hair on the hated head. Were one merely to seek information, one should inquire of the man who hates, but if one wishes to know what truly is, one better ask the one who loves.
Hermann Broch (1886–1951), Austrian writer

A good indignation brings out all of one's powers.
Ralph Waldo Emerson (1803–1882), American essayist and poet

Anger stirs and wakes in her; it opens its mouth, and like a hot-mouthed puppy, laps up the dredges of her shame. Anger is better. There is a sense of being in anger. A reality and presence. An awareness of worth.
Toni Morrison (b. 1931), American novelist

Had Narcissus himself seen his own face when he had been angry, he could never have fallen in love with himself.
Thomas Fuller (1608–1661), English clergyman

Anger dwells only in the bosom of fools.
Albert Einstein (1879–1955), German-born American physicist

I imagine one of the reasons people cling to their hate so stubbornly is because they sense, once hate is gone, they will be forced to deal with pain.
James Baldwin (1924–1987), American author

The tygers of wrath are wiser than the horses of instruction.
William Blake (1757–1827), English artist, poet, and mystic

Anger without power is folly.
German proverb

A sharp-tempered woman, or, for that matter, a man,
Is easier to deal with than the clever type
Who holds her tongue.
Euripides (480?–406? B.C.), Greek tragic playwright

Anger may be foolish and absurd, and one may be irritated when in the wrong; but a man never feels outraged unless in some respect he is at bottom right.
Victor Hugo (1802–1885), French author

Usually when people are sad, they don't do anything. But when they get angry, they bring about a change.
Malcolm X (1925–1965), American civil rights leader

He who doesn't know anger doesn't know anything. He doesn't know the immediate.
Henri Michaux (1899–1984), Belgian poet and painter

The bare recollection of anger rekindles anger.
Publilius Syrus (first century B.C.), Roman poet and actor

There is no old age for a man's anger,
Only death.
Sophocles (496?–406 B.C.), Greek tragic playwright

The malicious have a dark happiness.
Victor Hugo (1802–1885), French author

Anger raiseth invention, but it overheateth the oven.
Lord Halifax (1881–1959), English statesman

Hatred is settled anger.
Cicero (106–43 B.C.), Roman orator and philosopher

My loathings are simple: stupidity, oppression, crime, cruelty, soft music.
Vladimir Nabokov (1899–1977), Russian-born American novelist and poet

One should forgive one's enemies, but not before they are hanged.
Heinrich Heine (1797–1856), German lyric poet and literary critic

My hates have always occupied my mind much more actively and have given greater spiritual satisfaction than my friendships.
Westbrook Pegler (1894–1969), American columnist

I don't write polite letters. I don't like to plea-bargain. I like to fight.
Roy Cohn (1927–1986), American lawyer

You should make a woman angry if you wish her to love.
Publilius Syrus (first century B.C.), Roman poet and actor

A man should be careful not to raise the anger of a woman, for he has to sleep sometimes—and with his eyes closed.
Chinese proverb

Heaven has no rage, like love to hatred turned,
Nor Hell a fury, like a woman scorned.
William Congreve (1670–1729), English playwright

A man should study ever to keep cool. He makes his inferiors his superiors by heat.
Ralph Waldo Emerson (1803–1882), American essayist and poet

Be ye angry, and sin not: let not the sun go down upon your wrath.
The New Testament, Ephesians 4:26

We are told "Let not the sun go down on your wrath," but I would add, never act or write till it has done so. This rule has saved me from many an act of folly. It is wonderful what a different view we take of the same event four-and-twenty hours after it has happened.
Sydney Smith (1771–1845), English Anglican clergyman, essayist, and wit

Never go to bed mad. Stay up and fight.
Phyllis Diller (b. 1917), American comedian and actor

Anger repressed can poison a relationship as surely as the cruelest words.
Joyce Brothers (b. 1928), American psychoanalyst and author

If you must hate, if hatred is the leaven of your life, which alone can give flavor, then hate what should be hated: falsehood, violence, selfishness.
Ludwig Boerne (1786–1837), German political author and satirist

Take care that no one hate you justly.
Publilius Syrus (first century B.C.), Roman poet and actor

The fire you kindle for your enemy often burns yourself more than him.
Chinese proverb

Never settle with words what you can accomplish with a flamethrower.
Bruce Fierstein (b. 1953), American writer

How much more grievous are the consequences of anger than the causes of it.
Marcus Aurelius (121–180), Roman emperor and philosopher

Many promising reconciliations have broken down because, while both parties came prepared to forgive, neither party came prepared to be forgiven.
Charles Williams (1886–1945), English author

There is no such test of a man's superiority of character as in the well-conducting of an unavoidable quarrel.
Sir Henry Taylor (1800–1886), English author

Better be quarreling than lonesome.
Irish proverb

He who holds back rising anger like a rolling chariot, him I call a real driver; other people are but holding the reins.
Dhammapada (fifth century B.C.), Buddhist scripture

Anger deprives a sage of his wisdom, a prophet of his vision.
The Talmud

Reason opposes evil the more effectively when anger ministers at her side.
St. Gregory the Great (540–604)

As long as anger lives, she continues to be the fruitful mother of many unhappy children.
St. John Climacus (525–600), Christian saint

Anger, even violent anger, against one person will cease if vengeance is taken on another.
Aristotle (384–322 B.C.), Greek philosopher

Laughter cannot bring back what anger has driven away.
Japanese proverb

The anger of a good man lasts an instant; that of a meddler two hours; that of a base man a day and a night; and that of a great sinner until death.
Sanscrit proverb

In a fight, anger is as good as courage.
Welsh proverb

They exchanged the quick, brilliant smiles of women who dislike each other on sight.
Marshall Pugh (b. 1925), English author and journalist

The two women exchanged the kind of glance women use when no knife is handy.
Ellery Queen (Pseudonym of two cousins who wrote the Ellery Queen books—Frederic Dannay, 1905–1982; and Manfred B. Lee, 1905–1971)

Violent antipathies are always suspicious, and betray a secret affinity.
William Hazlitt (1778–1830), English essayist and critic

A lady of what is commonly called an uncertain temper—a phrase which being interpreted signifies a temper tolerably certain to make everybody more or less uncomfortable.
Charles Dickens (1812–1870), English novelist

Life appears to me too short to be spent in nursing animosity or registering wrong.
Charlotte Brontë (1816–1855), English novelist

An angry man opens his mouth and closes his eyes.
Cato the Elder (234–149 B.C.), Roman statesman

The intoxication of anger, like that of the grape, shows us to others, but hides us from ourselves. We injure our own cause in the opinion of the world when we too passionately defend it.
Charles Caleb Colton (1780–1832), English Anglican clergyman

Consider how much more you often suffer from your anger and grief, than from those very things for which you are angry and grieved.
Marcus Aurelius (121–180), Roman emperor and philosopher

The worst tempered people I've ever met were people who knew they were wrong.
Wilson Mizner (1876–1933), American author

It's far better to make people angry than to make them ashamed.
Sir Rabindranath Tagore (1861–1941), Hindu poet

The basest and meanest of all human beings are generally the most forward to despise others. So that the most contemptible are generally the most contemptuous.

Henry Fielding (1707–1754), English novelist and playwright

In doing good, we are generally cold, and languid, and sluggish; and of all things afraid of being too much in the right. But the works of malice and injustice are quite in another style. They are finished with a bold masterly hand, touched as they are with the spirit of those vehement passions that call forth all our energies whenever we oppress and persecute.

Edmund Burke (1729–1797), Irish-born English statesman and philosopher

An angry man is again angry with himself when he returns to reason.

Publilius Syrus (first century B.C.), Roman poet and actor

Man is a rational animal who always loses his temper when called upon to act in accordance with the dictates of reason.

Oscar Wilde (1854–1900), Irish poet, wit, and playwright

A tart temper never mellows with age, and a sharp tongue is the only edged tool that grows keener with constant use.

Washington Irving (1783–1859), American author

Love must be learned, and learned again and again; there is no end to it. Hate needs no instruction, but waits only to be provoked.

Katherine Anne Porter (1890–1980), American writer

Gentlemen: You have undertaken to cheat me. I won't sue you, for the law is too slow. I'll ruin you.

Cornelius Vanderbilt (1794–1877), American industrialist, in a letter written to a competitor

One man was so mad at me that he ended his letter: "Beware. You will never get out of this world alive."

John Steinbeck (1902–1968), American novelist

Hatred is so lasting and stubborn, that reconciliation on a sickbed certainly forebodes death.
Jean de La Bruyere (1645–1696), French essayist

Take away hatred from some people, and you have men without faith.
Eric Hoffer (1902–1983), American author

Anger represents a certain power, when a great mind, prevented from executing its own generous desires, is moved by it.
Pietro Aretino (1492–1556), Italian writer

The weak can never forgive. Forgiveness is the attribute of the strong.
Mahatma Gandhi (1869–1948), Indian political reformer

Only the brave know how to forgive. . . . A coward never forgave; it is not in his nature.
Laurence Sterne (1713–1768), English Anglican clergyman and novelist

Malice drinks one-half of its own poison.
Seneca (3? B.C.–A.D. 65?), Roman statesman and philosopher

Holding on to anger is like grasping a hot coal with the intent of throwing it at someone else; you are the one who gets burned.
Buddha (563?–483? B.C.), Indian religious leader

Anger is a killing thing: It kills the man who angers, for each rage leaves him less than he had been before—it takes something from him.
Louis L'Amour (1908–1988), American novelist

To be wronged is nothing unless you continue to remember it.
Confucius (551–479 B.C.), Chinese philosopher

Even the ancillary words, the names of anger's sidekicks, are a pleasure on the tongue. Spite, vengeance, rage. Just listen to the snaky "s," the acidic, arrowlike soft "g," the lucid, plosive "t" preceded by the chilled long "i," then dropped. The onomatopoeia of drawn swords. Nothing muffled, muffling, nothing concealing, nothing to protect the weak. To live in anger is to forget one was ever weak, to believe that what others call weakness is a sham, a feint that one exposes and removes, like the sanitizing immolation of a plague-ridden house. The cruelty essential for the nation's greater health, because, after all, the weak pull down the strong. The angry one is radiant in strength, and, blazing like the angel with the flaming sword, banishes the transgressors from the garden they would now only defile.
Mary Gordon (b. 1949), American author

In the souls of the people the grapes of wrath are filling and growing heavy, growing heavy for the vintage.
John Steinbeck (1902–1968), American novelist

All mourning fears its end and thinks with terror of the day when its pain will subside. In the same way, hate fears above all to be delivered of itself. Once more, it grips its tail between its teeth.
Hervé Bazin (b. 1911), French writer

Pure good soon grows insipid, wants variety and spirit. Pain is bitter-sweet, which never surfeits. Love turns, with a little indulgence, to indifference or disgust; hatred alone is immortal.
William Hazlitt (1778–1830), English essayist and critic

All men naturally hate one another. They employ lust as far as possible in the service of the public weal. But this is only a pretence and a false image of love; for at bottom it is only hate.
Blaise Pascal (1623–1662), English novelist and poet

Anger is not only inevitable, it is necessary. Its absence means indifference, the most disastrous of all human failings.
Arthur Ponsonby (1871–1946), English diplomat and writer

You want to hate somebody, if you can, just to keep your powers of discrimination bright, and to save yourself from becoming a mere mush of good-nature.
Charles Dudley Warner (1829–1900), American editor and author

If you hate a person, you hate something in him that is part of yourself. What isn't part of ourselves doesn't disturb us.
Hermann Hesse (1877–1962), German writer

Aggressiveness is the principal guarantor of survival.
Robert Ardrey (1908–1980), American writer

You cannot shake hands with a clenched fist.
Indira Gandhi (1917–1984), Indian prime minister

I am Wrath, I had neither father nor mother: I leap'd out of a lion's mouth when I was scarce half an hour old; and ever since I have run up and down the world with this case of rapiers, wounding myself when I had nobody to fight withal.
Christopher Marlowe (1564–1593), English playwright

There was never an angry man that thought his anger unjust.
Saint Francis De Sales (1567–1622), French Roman Catholic bishop and author

All anger is not sinful, because some degree of it, and on some occasions, is inevitable. But it becomes sinful and contradicts the rule of scripture when it is conceived upon slight and inadequate provocation, and when it continues long.

William Paley (1743–1805), English-American political philosopher and author

The mystery of our time is the inability of decent people to get angry. At present, anger and daring have become the monopoly of a band of mindless juvenile terrorists.

Eric Hoffer (1902–1983), American author

The most common of all antagonisms arises from a man's taking a seat beside you on the train, a seat to which he is completely entitled.

Robert Benchley (1889–1945), American humorist

Don't take the wrong side of an argument just because your opponent has taken the right side.

Baltasar Gracian (1601–1658), Spanish writer and Jesuit priest

It is a sin peculiar to man to hate his victim.

Tacitus (55?–120?), Roman orator, politician, and historian

You've got to know someone pretty well to hate them.

Bette Davis (1908–1989), American actor

No one delights more in vengeance than a woman.

Juvenal (60?–130?), Roman lawyer and satirist

There are some meannesses which are too mean even for man—woman, lovely woman alone, can venture to commit them.

William Makepeace Thackeray (1811–1863), English novelist

She intended to forgive. Not to do so would be un-Christian; but she did not intend to do so soon, nor forget how much she had to forgive.

Jessamyn West (1902–1984), American author

I loathe people who keep dogs. They are cowards who haven't got the guts to bite people themselves.

August Strindberg (1849–1912), Swedish playwright

Arguments only confirm people in their own opinions.

Booth Tarkington (1869–1946), American novelist

The moment you grab someone by the lapels, you're lost.

Burt Reynolds (b. 1936), American actor

In the fight between you and the world, back the world.

Franz Kafka (1883–1924), Austrian poet and author

Don't hit at all if it is honorably possible to avoid hitting; but *never* hit soft.

Theodore Roosevelt (1858–1919), twenty-sixth American president

Keep cool; anger is not an argument.

Daniel Webster (1782–1852), American orator, lawyer, and statesman

I think one of the great problems we have in the Republican Party is that we don't encourage you to be nasty. We encourage you to be neat, obedient, loyal and faithful and all those Boy Scout words, which would be great around a campfire but are lousy in politics.

Newt Gingrich (b. 1943), American congressman and House speaker

This is New York, and there's no law against being annoying.

William Kunstler (1919–1996), American lawyer and social activist

The first human being who hurled an insult instead of a stone was the founder of civilization.

Sigmund Freud (1856–1939), Austrian psychoanalyst

I don't know what will be used in the next world war, but the fourth will be fought with stones.

Albert Einstein (1879–1955), German-born American physicist

Anger is never without a reason but seldom a good one.

Benjamin Franklin (1706–1790), American statesman, scientist, and author

Seeing a murder on television can help work off one's antagonisms. And if you haven't any antagonisms, the commercials will give you some.

Alfred Hitchcock (1899–1980), English film director

We English are good at forgiving our enemies; it releases us from the obligation of liking our friends.

P. D. James (b. 1920), English novelist

Argument is the worst kind of conversation.

Jonathan Swift (1667–1745), Anglo-Irish author

The only way to succeed is to make people hate you. That way, they remember you.

Joseph Von Sternberg (1894–1969), Austrian-born American film director and actor

If you don't disagree with me, how will I know I'm right?

Samuel Goldwyn (1882–1974), Polish-born American film producer

To live is to war with trolls.

Henrik Ibsen (1828–1906), Norwegian poet and playwright

National hatred is something peculiar. You will always find it strongest and most violent where there is the lowest degree of culture.

Johann Wolfgang von Goethe (1749–1832), German poet and philosopher

In some cases non-violence requires more militancy than violence.

Cesar Chavez (1927–1993), American labor leader

The man who strikes first admits that his ideas have given out.

Chinese proverb

He who establishes his argument by noise and command, shows that his reason is weak.

Michel Eyquem de Montaigne (1553–1592), French essayist and courtier

The end move in politics is always to pick up a gun.

R. Buckminster Fuller (1895–1983), American architect, engineer, and theoretician

Love your enemies. It makes them so damned mad.

P. D. East (1921–1971), American author and editor

This is certain, that a man that studieth revenge keeps his wounds green, which otherwise would heal and do well.

Francis Bacon (1561–1626), English philosopher and author

Revenge leads to an empty fullness, like eating dirt.

Mignon McLaughlin (b. 1915), American writer

When I am right, I get angry. Churchill gets angry when he is wrong. So we were often angry at each other.

Charles de Gaulle (1890–1970), French general and president

Never ascribe to an opponent motives meaner than your own.

Sir J. M. Barrie (1860–1937), Scottish novelist and playwright

It is because people do not know each other that they hate each other so little.

Remy de Gourmont (1858–1915), French author and critic

Next to genius, nothing is more clear-sighted than hatred.

Claude Bernard (1813–1878), French physiologist

There is something about a roused woman . . . especially if she add to all her other strong passions the fierce impulses of recklessness and despair . . . which few men like to provoke.
Charles Dickens (1812–1870), English novelist

People who fly into rage always make a bad landing.
Will Rogers (1879–1935), American actor and humorist

A man that does not know how to be angry does not know how to be good.
Henry Ward Beecher (1813–1887), American congregational clergyman

Powerless rage can work miracles.
Stanislaw Lec (b. 1909), Polish poet

It takes two flints to make a fire.
Louisa May Alcott (1832–1888), American author

People who treat other people as less than human must not be surprised when the bread they have cast on the waters comes floating back to them, poisoned.
James Baldwin (1924–1987), American author

I love to see a young girl go out and grab the world by the lapels. Life's a bitch. You've got to go out and kick ass.
Maya Angelou (b. 1928), American author

To knock a thing down, especially if it is cocked at an arrogant angle, is a deep delight to the blood.
George Santayana (1863–1952), Spanish-born American poet and philosopher

Does our ferocity not derive from the fact that our instincts are all too interested in other people? If we attended more to ourselves and became the center, the object of our murderous inclinations, the sum of our intolerances would diminish.
E. M. Cioran (b. 1911), Rumanian-born French philosopher

To have a grievance is to have a purpose in life.
Eric Hoffer (1902–1983), American author

What we need is hatred. From it our ideas are born.
Jean Genet (1910–1986), French playwright and novelist

Aggression, the writer's main source of energy.
Ted Solotaroff (b. 1928), American editor

You gave him an opportunity of showing greatness of character and he did not seize it. He will never forgive you for that.
Friedrich Nietzsche (1844–1900), German philosopher

Hatred is an affair of the heart; *contempt* that of the head.
Arthur Schopenhauer (1788–1860), German philosopher

Whatever is begun in anger ends in shame.
Benjamin Franklin (1706–1790), American statesman, scientist, and author

Hatred, for the man who is engaged in it, is a little like the odor of garlic for one who hasn't eaten any.
Jean Rostand (1894–1977), French biologist and writer

The most deadly fruit is borne by the hatred which one grafts on an extinguished friendship.
Gotthold Ephraim Lessing (1729–1781), German philosopher and playwright

No one can be as calculatedly rude as the English, which amazes Americans, who do not understand studied insult and can only offer abuse as a substitute.
Paul Gallico (1897–1976), American novelist

Take care; you know I am compliance itself, when I am not thwarted! No one more easily led, when I have my own way; but don't put me in a phrenzy.
Richard Brinsley Sheridan (1751–1816), Irish-born English playwright

A man cannot be too careful in the choice of his enemies.
Oscar Wilde (1854–1900), Irish poet, wit, and playwright

The object of war is not to die for your country but to make the other bastard die for his.
General George Patton (1885–1945), American general

Friends may come and go, but enemies accumulate.
Thomas Jones (1892–1969), American sculptor

You can get more with a kind word and a gun than you can with a kind word alone.
Al Capone (1899–1947), American gangster

How can I lose to such an idiot?
A shout from chessmaster Aaron Nimzovich (1886–1935)

Why don't you write books people can read?
Nora Joyce to her husband, Irish writer James Joyce (1882–1941)

The right to swing my fist ends where the other man's nose begins.
Oliver Wendell Holmes (1841–1935), American jurist

There are glances of hatred that stab, and raise no cry of murder.
George Eliot (1819–1880), English novelist

What do you despise? By this are you truly known.
Frank Herbert (1920–1986), American writer

Hell will never have its due till it have you.
Thomas Fuller (1608–1661), English clergyman

No matter what side of the argument you are on, you always find people that you wish were on the other side.
Jascha Heifitz (1901–1987), Russian-born American violinist

If you cannot answer a man's argument, all is not lost, you can still call him vile names.
Elbert Hubbard (1856–1915), American author and editor

The adjective "cross" as a description of his Jovelike wrath . . . jarred upon Derek profoundly. It was as though Prometheus, with the vultures tearing his liver, had been asked if he were piqued.
P. G. Wodehouse (1881–1975), English novelist and humorist

It's my rule never to lose me temper till it would be detrimental to keep it.
Sean O'Casey (1880–1964), Irish playwright

People who know the least always argue the most.
Anonymous

At this present moment, I have the strong urge to go over there, wrap both his legs round his neck and stick his suede shoes in his mouth. But I suppose that would be termed a temporary solution.
Alan Ayckbourn (b. 1939), English playwright

If you are patient in one moment of anger, you will escape a hundred days of sorrow.
Chinese proverb

Men's arguments often prove nothing but their wishes.
Charles Caleb Colton (1780–1832), English Anglican clergyman

Fear not those who argue, but those who dodge.
Marie von Ebner-Eschenbach (1830–1916), Austrian novelist and poet

He that blows the coals in quarrels that he has nothing to do with, has no right to complain if sparks fly in his face.
Benjamin Franklin (1706–1790), American statesman, inventor, and writer

A lot of good arguments are spoiled by some damn fool who knows what he's talking about.
Anonymous

I have suckled the wolf's lip of anger. I have used it for illumination, laughter, protection, fire in places where there was no light, no food, no sisters, no quarter.

Audre Lorde (1934–1992), West Indies–born American poet, writer, and educator

Cruelty, like every other vice, requires no motive outside itself; it only requires opportunity.

George Eliot (1819–1880), English novelist

"I can forgive, but I cannot forget" is only another way of saying, "I will not forgive." Forgiveness ought to be like a canceled note—torn in two and burned up so that it never can be shown against one.

Henry Ward Beecher (1813–1887), American congregational clergyman

In quarreling, the truth is always lost.

Publilius Syrus (first century B.C.), Roman poet and actor

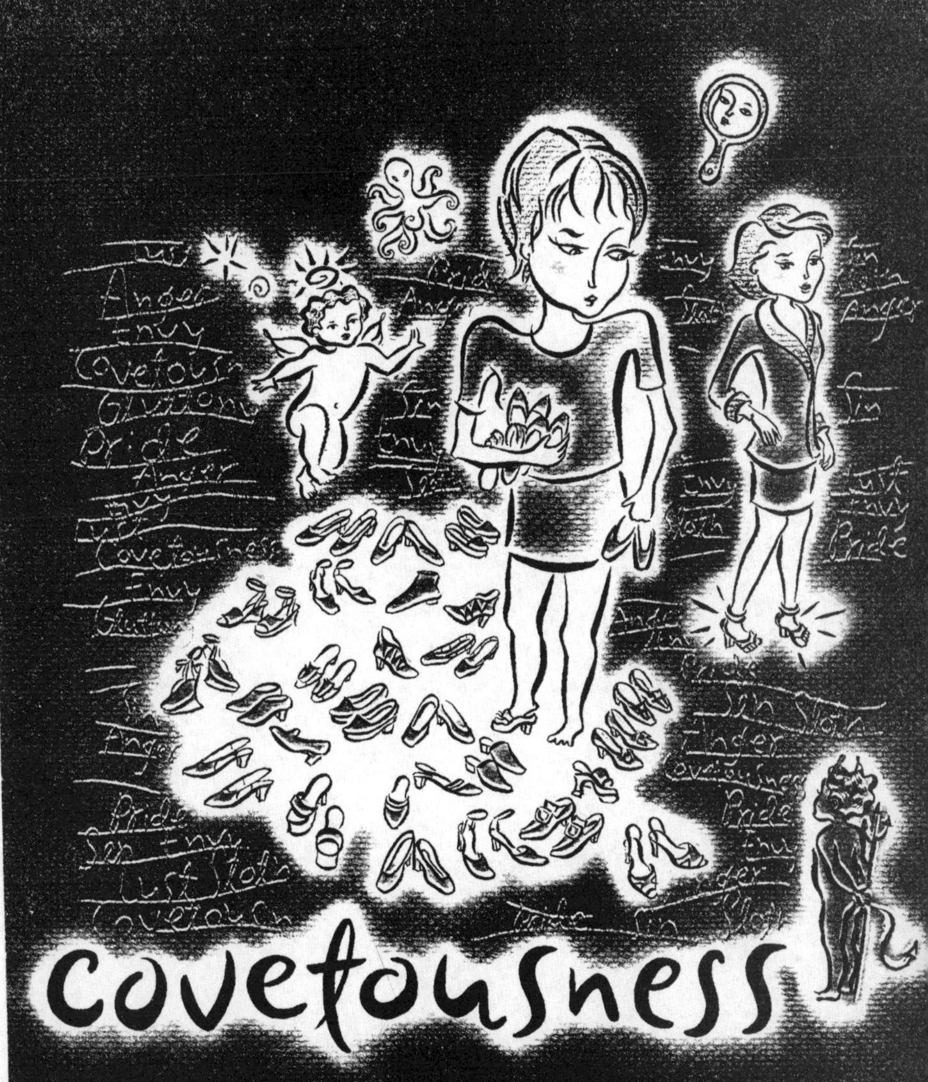
Covetousness

Covetousness

Sin: Covetousness

Definition: (kə'-və-təs-nuss), *n.* 1. inordinately or wrongfully desirous.

See: greed; rapacity; resentfulness; spitefulness; possessiveness; protectiveness; suspiciousness; malevolence; rancor; vengefulness; malice; vindictiveness; acquisitiveness; eagerness; usury; self-consideration; self-love; egocentricity; venality; insatiability; money-madness; unquenchability; tightfistedness; unappeasability; graspiness; retentiveness; mean-mindedness; self-aggrandizement; cupidity; pettiness; meanness; avidity; hoggishness; keenness; voracity; selfishness; grabbiness; thirstiness

See also: begrudge; choose; fancy; hope; long; hanker; ask; desire; need; want; ache; crave; itch; pant; wish; pine; yearn; cadge; require; favor; prefer; clutch at; money-grub; promise oneself; have an eye on; set one's heart on; spoil for; angle for; have a yen for; have the hots for; cry out for; clamor for; fish for; gasp for; burn for; die for; shoot for the moon; be keen; be mercenary; be uncharitable; be penurious; be unsated; be omnivorous; be open-mouthed; be grudging; be piggish; be avaricious; be ravenous; be miserly; be self-seeking; be self-serving; be self-interested; be pinching; be prehensile; be green-eyed; be ungenerous; be unslaked

A private railroad car is not an acquired taste. One takes to it immediately.
Eleanor Robson Belmont (1879–1979), English-born American actor and philanthropist

Money isn't everything, your health is the other ten percent.
Lillian Day (1893–1991), English writer

Money, it turned out, was exactly like sex, you thought of nothing else if you didn't have it and thought of other things if you did.
James Baldwin (1924–1987), American author

See here: when you speak the word *avarice*, when you utter the verb *to have*, feel how fondly your front teeth caress your lower lip; that is how the meaning comes, our bodies making out, making up the sense of the words. . . Our senses make it: *avid*! my friend, as eager to own the self as the mouth to own the tongue.
Richard Howard (b. 1929), American writer

We're all born brave, trusting and greedy, and most of us remain greedy.
Mignon McLaughlin (b. 1930), American writer

I did not have three thousand pairs of shoes, I had one thousand and sixty.
Imelda Marcos (b. 1930), wife of Ferdinand Marcos, ousted Philippine dictator

Better to be nouveau than never to have been rich at all.
Anonymous

I know him [greed]. He's a good old son of a bitch.
Billy Carter (1937–1988), brother of president Jimmy Carter

Even those who appear to take nothing seriously take their greed . . . seriously.
Dr. Michael Maccoby (b. 1933), American educator and writer

The things we are best acquainted with are often the things we lack. This is because we have spent so much time thinking of them.
Gerald Brenan (1894–1987), English writer

An aspiration is a joy forever, a possession as solid as a landed estate.
Robert Louis Stevenson (1850–1894), Scottish writer

The value of a thing sometimes lies not in what one attains with it, but in what one pays for it—what it *costs* us.
Friedrich Nietzsche (1844–1900), German philosopher and poet

An animal needing something knows how much it needs, the man does not.
Democritus of Abders (460?–370? B.C.), Greek philosopher

Avarice is generally the last passion of those lives of which the first part has been squandered in pleasure, and the second devoted to ambition.
Samuel Johnson (1709–1784), English author

I don't know much about being a millionaire, but I'll bet I'd be darling at it.
Dorothy Parker (1893–1967), American author

The love of money is the root of all evil.
The New Testament, 1 Timothy 6:10

Lack of money is the root of all evil.
George Bernard Shaw (1856–1950), Irish playwright, author, and critic

Perhaps you will say a man is not young; I answer, he is rich; he is not gentle, handsome, witty, brave, good-humored, but he is rich, rich, rich, rich, rich—that one word contradicts everything you can say against him.
Henry Fielding (1707–1754), English novelist and playwright

To be clever enough to get all that money, one must be stupid enough to want it.
G. K. Chesterton (1874–1936), English journalist and author

You have to decide whether you want to make money or make sense, because the two are mutually exclusive.
R. Buckminster Fuller (1895–1983), American architect, engineer, and theoretician

So for a good old-gentlemanly vice,
I think I must take up with avarice.
Lord Byron (1788–1824), English poet

Greed is all right, by the way . . . I think greed is healthy. You can be greedy and still feel good about yourself.
Ivan Boesky (b. 1937), American businessman

The point is, you can't be too greedy.
Donald Trump (b. 1946), American real estate developer

Do not your inclinations tell you that the *world* is yours? Do you not covet all? Do you not long to have it; to enjoy it; to overcome it? To what end do men gather riches, but to multiply more? Do they not like Pyrrhus the King of Epire, add house to house and lands to lands, that they might get it all?
Thomas Traherne (1636–1674), English poet and clergyman

You have no idea how promising the world begins to look once you have decided to have it all for yourself. And how much healthier your decisions are once they become entirely selfish.

Anita Brookner (b. 1938), English art historian and novelist

Consider any individual at any period of his life, and you will always find him preoccupied with fresh plans to increase his comfort. Do not talk to him about the interests and rights of the human race; that little private business of his for the moment absorbs all his thoughts, and he hopes that public disturbances can be put off to some other time.

Alexis de Tocqueville (1805–1859), French historian

The war [World War II], which destroyed so much of everything, was also constructive, in a way. It established clearly the cold, and finally unhypocritical fact that the most important thing on earth to men today is money.

Janet Flanner (1892–1978), American journalist and novelist

There are a handful of people whom money won't spoil, and we all count ourselves among them.

Mignon McLaughlin (b. 1930), American writer

I believe only in money, not in love or tenderness. Love and tenderness meant only pain and suffering and defeat. I would not let it ruin me as it ruined others! I would speak only with money, hard money.

Agnes Smedley (1894?–1950), American author and journalistr

Money creates taste.

Jenny Holzer (b. 1950), American artist

You don't seem to realize that a poor person who is unhappy is in a better position than a rich person who is unhappy. Because the poor person has hope. He thinks money would help.

Jean Kerr (b. 1923), American author and playwright

The pleasure of possession, whether we possess trinkets or offspring—or possibly books, or chessmen, or stamps—lies in showing these things to friends who are experiencing no immediate urge to look at them.

Agnes Repplier (1855–1950), American essayist

Spoiled. That's all it's about—can't live without this, can't live without that. You can live without anything you weren't born with, and you can make it through on even half of that.

Gloria Naylor (b. 1950), American author

No one in this world needs a mink coat but a mink.

Anonymous

Poverty makes me feel weak, as if I were coming down with an awful debilitating, communicable disease—the disease of being without money. Instead of going to the hospital, you went to the poor farm. The difference was, you never got well at the poor farm.

Faith Sullivan (b. 1933), American author

You don't want no pie in the sky when
you die,
You want something here on the
ground while you're still around.

Muhammad Ali (b. 1942), American boxing champion

Years ago a person, he was unhappy, didn't know what to do with himself—he'd go to church, start a revolution—*something*. Today you're unhappy? Can't figure it out? What is the salvation? Go shopping.

Arthur Miller (b. 1915), American playwright

Anyone informed that the universe is expanding and contracting in pulsations of eighty billion years has a right to ask, "What's in it for me?"

Peter De Vries (1910–1993), American author

It is difficult to love mankind unless one has a reasonable private income and when one has a reasonable private income one has better things to do than loving mankind.

Hugh Kingsmill (1889–1949), English writer

Thinking to get at once all the gold that the goose could give, he killed it, and opened it only to find—nothing.

Aesop (sixth century B.C.), supposed author of Greek fables

A gold rush is what happens when a line of chorus girls spot a man with a bank roll.

Mae West (1892–1980), American actor

I must say I hate money but it's the lack of it I hate most.

Katherine Mansfield (1888–1923), English author

Nothing retains less of desire in art, in science, than this will to industry, booty, possession.

André Breton (1896–1966), French poet and essayist (founder of surrealism)

Young people everywhere have been allowed to choose between love and a garbage disposal unit. Everywhere they have chosen the garbage disposal unit.

Guy Debord (b. 1931), French philosopher

Once one is caught up into the material world not one person in ten thousand finds the time to form literary taste, to examine the validity of philosophic concepts for himself, or to form what, for lack of a better phrase, I might call the wise and tragic sense of life.
F. Scott Fitzgerald (1896–1940), American author

When I am a rich man with my own bicycle and can have beer for breakfast, I shall give up writing poetry all together.
Dylan Thomas (1914–1953), Welsh poet

When we of the so-called better classes are scared as men were never scared in history at material ugliness and hardship; when we put off marriage until our house can be artistic, and quake at the thought of having a child without a bank-account and doomed to manual labor, it is time for thinking men to protest against so unmanly and irreligious a state of opinion.
William James (1842–1910), American psychologist and philosopher

Any so-called material thing that you want is merely a symbol: you want it not for *itself*, but because it will content your spirit for the moment.
Mark Twain (1835–1910), American writer

Money doesn't always bring happiness. A man with ten million dollars is no happier than a man with nine million dollars.
Anonymous

When I was young I used to think that money was the most important thing in life; now that I am old I know it is.
Oscar Wilde (1854–1900), Irish poet, wit, and playwright

God shows his contempt for wealth by the kind of person he selects to receive it.
Austin O'Malley (1858–1932), American physician and author

[Riches are] a gift from Heaven signifying, "This is my beloved son, in whom I am well pleased."
John D. Rockefeller (1839–1937), American financier

I have enough money to last me the rest of my life, unless I buy something.
Jackie Mason (b. 1931), American comedian

Why is there so much month left at the end of the money?
Maurice Chevalier (1888–1972), French actor and singer

It is a kind of spiritual snobbery that makes people think they can be happy without money.
Albert Camus (1913–1960), French existentialist author

It doesn't matter whether you are rich or poor—as long as you've got money.
Joe E. Lewis (1902–1971), American actor and comedian

Man must choose whether to be rich in things or in the freedom to use them.
Ivan Illich (b. 1926), Austrian-born American theologian and author

This country can seduce God. Yes, it has that seductive power—the power of dollarism.
Malcolm X (1925–1965), American civil rights leader

Here was a new generation . . . dedicated more than the last to the fear of poverty and the worship of success; grown up to find all the gods dead, all wars fought, all faiths in man shaken.
F. Scott Fitzgerald (1896–1940), American author

Superfluous wealth can buy superfluities only.
Henry David Thoreau (1817–1862), American author and naturalist

After hypocrites, the greatest dupes the devil has are those who exhaust an anxious existence in the disappointments and vexations of business, and live miserably and meanly only to die magnificently and rich. They serve the devil without receiving his wages, and for the empty foolery of dying rich, pay down their health, happiness, and integrity.
Charles Caleb Colton (1780?–1832), English Anglican clergyman

When all sins are old in us and go upon crutches, covetousness does then but lie in her cradle.
Thomas Dekker (1570–1641), English playwright

Refrain from covetousness, and thy estate shall prosper.
Plato (429–347 B.C.), Greek philosopher

Covetousness is both the beginning and end of the devil's alphabet—the first vice in corrupt nature that moves, and the last which dies.
Robert South (1634–1716), English court preacher

Men living in democratic times have many passions, but most of their passions either end in the love of riches, or proceed from it.
Alexis de Tocqueville (1805–1859), French historian

What nature requires is obtainable, and within easy reach. It's for the superfluous we sweat.
Lucius Annaeus Seneca (3 B.C.?–A.D. 65?), Roman statesman and philosopher

I know it is more agreeable to walk upon carpets than to lie upon dungeon floors; I know it is pleasant to have all the comforts and luxuries of civilization; but he who cares only for these things is worth no more than a butterfly contented and thoughtless upon a morning flower; and who ever thought of rearing a tombstone to a last-summer's butterfly?
Henry Ward Beecher (1813–1887), American congregational clergyman

Unless we are accustomed to them from early youth, splendid chambers and elegant furniture had best be left to people who neither have nor can have any thoughts.
Johann Wolfgang von Goethe (1749–1832), German poet and philosopher

Many priceless things can be bought.
Marie von Ebner-Eschenbach (1830–1916), Austrian novelist and poet

Those who have some means think that the most important thing in the world is love. The poor know it is money.
Gerald Brenan (1894–1987), English writer

Liking money like I like it, is nothing less than mysticism. Money is a glory.
Salvador Dalí (1904–1989), Spanish surrealist artist

If money be not thy servant, it will be thy master. The covetous man cannot so properly be said to possess wealth, as that may be said to possess him.
Francis Bacon (1561–1626), English philosopher and author

Garrick showed Johnson his fine house, gardens, statues, pictures, etc., at Hampton Court. "Ah! David, David," said the doctor, "these are the things that make death terrible."
Julius Bate (1711–1771), English Anglican clergyman

The most valuable of all human possessions, next to a superior and disdainful air, is the reputation of being well to do. Nothing else so neatly eases one's way through life, especially in democratic countries.
H. L. Mencken (1880–1956), American satirist and editor

Every man who is worth thirty millions and is not wedded to them, is dangerous to the government.
Napoleon Bonaparte (1769–1821), French emperor

The makers of fortunes have a second love of money as a creation of their own, resembling the affection of authors for their own poems, or of parents for their children, besides that natural love of it for the sake of use and profit.
Plato (429–347 B.C.), Greek philosopher

All else—valor, a good name, glory, everything in heaven and earth—is secondary to the charm of riches.
Horace (65–68 B.C.), Roman poet

Majestic mighty Wealth is the holiest of our gods.
Juvenal (60?–130?), Roman lawyer and satirist

HAND, *n.* A singular instrument worn at the end of a human arm and commonly thrust into somebody's pocket.
Ambrose Bierce (1842–1914), American writer

It is easy to get everything you want, provided you first learn to do without the things you cannot get.
Elbert Hubbard (1856–1915), American author and editor

The collector walks with blinders on; he sees nothing but the prize. In fact, the acquisitive instinct is incompatible with true appreciation of beauty.
Anne Morrow Lindbergh (b. 1906), American writer

All heiresses are beautiful.
John Dryden (1631–1700), English poet

Greed is a bottomless pit which exhausts the person in an endless effort to satisfy the need without ever reaching satisfaction.
Erich Fromm (1900–1980), German-born American psychoanalyst

Avarice is a fine, absorbin' passion, an' manny an ol' fellow is as happy with his arm around his bank account as he was sleigh ridin' with his first girl.
Finley Peter Dunne (1867–1936), American humorist

People who are greedy have extraordinary capacities for waste—they must, they take in too much.
Norman Mailer (b. 1923), American writer

I could not possibly count the gold-digging ruses of women,
Not if I had ten mouths, not if I had ten mouths.
Ovid (43 B.C.–A.D. 17), Roman poet

Though avarice will prevent a man from being necessitously poor, it generally makes him too timorous to be wealthy.
Thomas Paine (1737–1809), English-American political philosopher and author

Avarice is as destitute of what it has, as poverty of what it has not.

Publilius Syrus (first century B.C.), Roman poet and actor

For greed all nature is too little.

Lucius Annaeus Seneca (3 B.C.?–A.D. 65?), Roman statesman and philosopher

To have money is to be virtuous, honest, beautiful and witty. And to be without is to be ugly and boring and stupid and useless.

Jean Giraudoux (1882–1944), French playwright, novelist, essayist, and diplomat

With his own money a person can live as he likes—a ruble that's your own is dearer than your brother.

Maxim Gorky (1868–1936), Russian writer

Some men make money not for the
sake of living, but ache
In the blindness of greed and live just
for their fortune's sake.

Juvenal (60?–130?), Roman lawyer and satirist

Money is like a sixth sense without which you cannot make a complete use of the other five.

W. Somerset Maugham (1874–1965), English novelist and playwright

Life is short and so is money.

Bertolt Brecht (1898–1956), German poet and playwright

Cultivated people should be superior to any consideration as sordid as a mercenary interest.

Molière (1622–1673), French actor and playwright

He that has a penny in his purse, is worth a penny: Have and you shall be esteemed.

Gaius Petronius (first century A.D.), probable author of the Satyricon

Give us the luxuries of life, and we will dispense with its necessities.

John Lothrop Motley (1814–1877), American historian

The force of the guineas you have in your pocket depends wholly on the default of a guinea in your neighbour's pocket. If he did not want it, it would be of no use to you.

John Ruskin (1819–1900), English author and critic

With money in your pocket, you are wise and you are handsome and you sing well too.

Yiddish proverb

Money is power, freedom, a cushion, the root of all evil. The sum of blessings.

Carl Sandburg (1878–1967), American poet and novelist

There was a time when a fool and his money were soon parted, but now it happens to everybody.
Adlai Stevenson (1900–1965), American politician

It isn't enough for you to love money—it's also necessary that money should love you.
Baron Rothschild (1808–1879), English banker

Money is the most egalitarian force in society. It confers power on whomever holds it.
Roger Starr (b. 1918), American author

I don't like money actually, but it quiets my nerves.
Joe Louis (1914–1981), American boxing champion

If the rich could hire other people to die for them, the poor would make a wonderful living.
Jewish proverb

Gentlemen prefer bonds.
Andrew Mellon (1855–1937), American financier

Covetousness has for its mother unlawful desire, for its daughter injustice, and for its friend violence.
Arabian proverb

Money is just what we use to keep tally.
Henry Ford (1863–1947), American automobile manufacturer

Ambition is but avarice on stilts, and masked.
Walter Savage Landor (1775–1864), English author

Someday I want to be rich. Some people get so rich they lose all respect for humanity. That's how rich I want to be.
Rita Rudner (b. 1965), American comedian and actor

If I can't have too many truffles I'll do without.
Colette (1873–1954), French writer

A single woman with a narrow income must be a ridiculous old maid, the proper sport of boys and girls; but a single woman of good fortune is always respectable, and may be as sensible and pleasant as anybody else.
Jane Austen (1775–1817), English novelist

I don't know how it happens, my car just drives itself to Neiman Marcus.
Victoria Principal (b. 1950), American actor

I was street smart—but unfortunately the street was Rodeo Drive.
Carrie Fisher (b. 1956), American actor and writer

I'd like to be rich enough so I could throw soap away after the letters are worn off.

Andy Rooney (b. 1919), print, radio, and television commentator

I'd like to have money. And I'd like to be a good writer. These two can come together, and I hope they will, but if that's too adorable, I'd rather have money.

Dorothy Parker (1893–1967), American author

I'd like to live like a poor man with lots of money.

Pablo Picasso (1881–1973), Spanish painter and sculptor

I don't write for art's sake. I write for money.

Mickey Spillane (b. 1918), American writer

The only reason I'm in Hollywood is that I don't have the moral courage to refuse the money.

Marlon Brando (b. 1924), American actor

I did it for the loot, honey, always the loot.

Ava Gardner (1922–1990), American actor

I have a lust for diamonds, almost like a disease.

Elizabeth Taylor (b. 1932), English-born American film star

I've been in trouble most of my life; I've done the most unutterable rubbish, all because of money. I didn't need it . . . the lure of the zeros was simply too great.

Richard Burton (1925–1984), English actor

I'm tired of Love: I'm still more tired
of Rhyme
But Money gives me pleasure all
the time.

Hilaire Belloc (1870–1953), French-born English author

I went into the business for the money, and the art grew out of it. If people are disillusioned by that remark, I can't help it. It's the truth.

Charlie Chaplin (1889–1977), English actor and director

Anything that won't sell, I don't want to invent.

Thomas A. Edison (1847–1931), American inventor

Somebody said to me, "But the Beatles were anti-materialistic." That's a huge myth. John and I literally used to sit down and say, "Now, let's write a swimming pool."

Paul McCartney (b. 1942), musician and songwriter, former member of the Beatles

I am not rich. I am a poor man with money, which is not the same thing.

Gabriel García Márquez (b. 1928), Colombian-born American novelist

When I was young, I used to think that wealth and power would bring me happiness. I was right.

Gahan Wilson (b. 1930), American cartoonist and writer

Never steal more than you actually need, for the possession of surplus money leads to extravagance, foppish attire, frivolous thought.

Dalton Trumbo (1905–1976), American screenwriter

If you think the United States has stood still, who built the largest shopping center in the world?

Richard M. Nixon (1913–1994), thirty-seventh American president

Do you know what the country needs today? A seven-cent nickel. . . . If it works out, next year we could have an eight-cent nickel. . . . You could go to the newsstand, buy a three-cent newspaper and get the same nickel back again. One nickel carefully used would last a family a lifetime.

Groucho Marx (1890–1977), American film and television comedian

[Greed is] the lust for comfort, that stealthy thing that enters the house as a guest, and then becomes a host, and then a master.

Kahlil Gibran (1883–1931), Lebanese writer and poet

God is on everyone's side. . . . And, in the last analysis, he is on the side of those with plenty of money and large armies.

Jean Anouilh (1910–1987), French playwright

What female heart can gold despise? What cat's averse to fish?

Thomas Gray (1716–1771), English poet

To the eyes of a miser a guinea is far more beautiful than the sun, and a bag worn with the use of money has more beautiful proportions than a vine filled with grapes. The tree which moves some to tears of joy is in the eyes of others only a green thing which stands in the way. So a man is, so he sees.

William Blake (1757–1827), English artist, poet, and mystic

Money is human happiness in the abstract: he, then, who is no longer capable of enjoying human happiness in the concrete devotes himself utterly to money.

Arthur Schopenhauer (1788–1860), German philosopher

When I lack money, I'm bashful wherever I go. I must absolutely get over this. The best way would be to carry a hundred gold louis in my pocket every day for a year. The constant weight of the gold would destroy the root of the evil.
Henri Beyle Stendhal (1783–1842), French author

Trust your husband, adore your husband, and get as much as you can in your own name.
Joan Rivers (b. 1935), American comedian, quoting her mother

Lust of possession, prestige and power have also burned their devastating way into the very citadels of our civilization and have not been afraid to invade our sanctuaries.
Federal Council of Churches of Christ in America, 1932

He that serves God for money will serve the Devil for better wages.
Sir Roger L'Estrange (1616–1704), English journalist

He that is of the opinion money will do everything may well be suspected of doing everything for money.
Benjamin Franklin (1706–1790), American statesman, scientist, author

Money is life to us wretched mortals.
Hesiod (eighth century B.C.), Greek poet

You ought to have money. If you can honestly attain unto riches in Philadelphia, it is your Christian and godly duty to do so. It is an awful mistake of those pious people to think you must be awfully poor in order to be pious.
Russell H. Conwell (1843–1925), American cleric and educator

Whatever is not nailed down is mine. Whatever I can pry loose is not nailed down.
Oscar Wilde (1854–1900), Irish poet, wit, and playwright

Thou shalt not covet thy neighbor's house, thou shalt not covet thy neighbor's wife, nor his manservant, nor his maidservant, nor his ox, nor his ass, nor anything that is your neighbor's.
The Old Testament, Exodus 20:17

He was such a covetous monster that he would have flayed a louse to save the skin of it.
John Florio (1553?–1625), English author

The populace may hiss me, but when I go home and think of my money I applaud myself.
Horace (65–68 B.C.), Roman poet and satirist

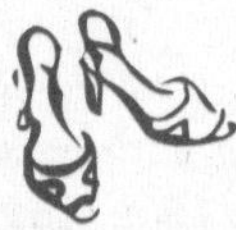

I am Covetousness, begotten of an old churl in an old leathern bag; and might I have my wish, I would desire that this house and all the people in it were turn'd to gold, that I might lock you up in my good chest.
Christopher Marlowe (1564–1593), English playwright

Bare-faced covetousness was the moving spirit of civilization from its first dawn to the present day; wealth, and again wealth, and for the third time wealth; wealth, not of society, but of the puny individual, was its only and final aim.
Friedrich Engels (1820–1895), German social philosopher

Money is mourned with deeper sorrow than friends or kindred.
Juvenal (60?–130?), Roman lawyer and satirist

Let us keep a firm grip upon our money, for without it the whole assembly of virtues are but as blades of grass.
Bharitihari (first century A.D.), Indian grammarian

O money, money, how blindly thou hast been worshipped, and how stupidly abused! Thou art health, and liberty, and strength; and he that has thee may rattle his pockets at the foul fiend.
Charles Lamb (1775–1834), English essayist and critic

A feast is made for laughter, and wine maketh merry. But money answereth all things.
The Old Testament, Ecclesiastes 10:19

It takes a kind of genius to make a fortune, and especially a large fortune. It is neither goodness, nor wit, nor talent, nor strength, nor delicacy. I don't know precisely what it is: I am waiting for some one to tell me.
Jean de la Bruyère (1645–1696), French essayist

When you are skinning your customers you should leave some skin on to grow again so that you can skin them again.
Nikita Krushchev (1894–1971), Russian premier, advising English businessmen

Every crowd has a silver lining.
Phineas T. Barnum (1810–1891), American showman

Money is the fruit of evil as often as the root of it.
Henry Fielding (1707–1754), English novelist and playwright

Money is the root of all evil, and yet it is such a useful root that we cannot get on without it any more than we can without potatoes.
Louisa May Alcott (1832–1888), American author

Living in the lap of luxury isn't bad, except you never know when luxury is going to stand up.
Orson Welles (1915–1985), American actor, director, and producer

Money is a singular thing. It ranks with love as man's greatest source of joy. And with death as his greatest source of anxiety. Money differs from an automobile, a mistress or cancer in being equally important to those who have it and those who do not.
John Kenneth Galbraith (b. 1908), Canadian-born American economist and educator

The people came to realize that wealth is not the fruit of labor but the result of organized protected robbery. Rich people are no longer respectable people; they are nothing more than flesh-eating animals, jackals and vultures which wallow in the people's blood.
Frantz Fanon (1925–1961), Martiniquan psychiatrist, philosopher, and political activist

He must have killed a lot of men to have made so much money.
Molière (1622–1673), French playwright

It's no fun being rich anymore. People are too damned jealous and suspicious of you. They figure that anybody that makes as much money as I allegedly have must have cheated somebody.
John D. Rockefeller (1839–1937), American financier

If you can actually count your money then you are not really a rich man.
J. Paul Getty (1892–1976), American oil magnate

The avaricious man is like the barren sandy ground of the desert which sucks in all the rain and dew with greediness, but yields no fruitful herbs or plants for the benefit of others.
Zeno of Citium (335?–263? B.C.), Greek philosopher

Few men have virtue to withstand the highest bidder.
George Washington (1732–1799), first American president

It is difficult to get a man to understand something when his salary depends upon his not understanding it.
Upton Sinclair (1878–1968), American author and reformer

The secret point of money and power in America is neither the things that money can buy nor power for power's sake . . . but absolute personal freedom, mobility, privacy. It is the instinct which drove America to the Pacific, all through the nineteenth century, the desire to be able to find a restaurant open in case you want a sandwich, to be a free agent, live by one's own rules.
Joan Didion (b. 1934), American writer

Many of the greatest creations of man have been inspired by the desire to make money. When George Frederick Handel was on his beam ends, he shut himself up for twenty-one days and emerged with the complete score of *Messiah*—and hit the jackpot.
David Mackenzie Ogilvy (b. 1911), British-born American advertising executive

Only the little people pay taxes.
Leona Helmsley (b. 1920), American businesswoman

Greed's worst point is its ingratitude.
Lucius Annaeus Seneca (3 B.C.?–A.D. 65?), Roman statesman and philosopher

Whoever does not regard what he has as most ample wealth is unhappy, though he is master of the world.
Epicurus (341–270 B.C.), Greek philosopher

Chastise your passions, that they may not chastise you. No one who is a lover of money, of pleasure, or of glory, is likewise a lover of mankind. Riches are not among the number of things that are good. It is not poverty that causes sorrow, but covetous desires. Deliver yourself from appetite, and you will be free. He who is discontented with things present and allotted, is unskilled in life.
Epictetus (A.D. 55?–135?), Greek stoic philosopher

Get place and wealth, if possible,
with grace;
If not, by any means get wealth and
place.
Alexander Pope (1688–1744), English poet

Of all the people in the world, those who want the most are those who have the most.
David Grayson (1870–1946), American journalist and author

Want is a growing giant whom the coat of Have was never large enough to cover.
Ralph Waldo Emerson (1803–1882), American essayist and poet

We are no longer happy so soon as we wish to be happier.
Walter Savage Landor (1775–1864), English author

He is not rich that possesses much, but he that covets no more; and he is not poor that enjoys little, but he that wants too much.

Francis Beaumont (1584–1616), English playwright

The only incurable troubles of the rich are the troubles that money can't cure.

Ogden Nash (1902–1971), American poet

All progress is based upon a universal, innate desire on the part of every living organism to live beyond its income.

Samuel Butler (1835–1902), English author

In our culture we make heroes of the men who sit on top of a heap of money, and we pay attention not only to what they say in their field of competence, but to their wisdom on every other question in the world.

Max Lerner (b. 1902), Russian-born American author and educator

It is extraordinary how many emotional storms one may weather in safety if one is ballasted with ever so little gold.

William McFee (1881–1966), American author

Money writes books, money sells them. Give me not righteousness, O Lord, give me money, only money.

George Orwell (1903–1950), American writer

I began to think of F. Scott Fitzgerald, the only writer this country had ever produced who knew to the last dollar and cent the moral worth of money.

Diana Trilling (1905–1996), American writer and critic

It is better to have a permanent income than to be fascinating.

Oscar Wilde (1854–1900), Irish poet, wit, and playwright

Money, big money (which is actually a relative concept) is always, under any circumstances, a seduction, a test of morals, a temptation to sin.

Boris Yeltsin (b. 1931), Russian president

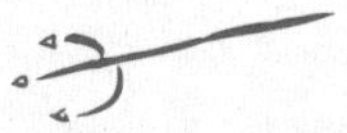

In every well-governed state, wealth is a sacred thing; in democracies it is the only sacred thing.

Anatole France (1844–1924), French writer

I am more and more convinced that man is a dangerous creature; and that power, whether vested in many or a few, is ever grasping, and, like the grave, cries, "Give, give!"

Abigail Adams (1744–1818), American writer and first lady to John Adams, second American president

Gold is a wonderful clearer of the understanding; it dissipates every doubt and scruple in an instant, accommodates itself to the meanest capacities, silences the loud and clamorous, and brings over the most obstinate and inflexible.

Joseph Addison (1672–1719), English essayist

What is the chief end of man?—to get rich. In what way?—dishonestly if he can; honestly if he must.

Mark Twain (1835–1910), American writer

He is bound fast by his wealth . . . his money owns him rather than he owns it.

Saint Cyprian (200–258), bishop of Carthage

All things obey money.

Desiderius Erasmus (1466?–1536), Dutch scholar

The only vice that I perceive in the universe is *Avarice*; all the others, whatever name they be known by, are only variations, degrees, of this one.

Morelly (Eighteenth century), French utopian philosopher

I buy newspapers to make money to buy more newspapers to make money. As for editorial content, that's the stuff you separate ads with.

Roy Thompson (1894–1977), English press lord

A heavy purse makes a light heart.

Sixteenth-century English proverb

Business! I think that there is nothing, not even crime, more opposed to poetry, to philosophy, ay, to life itself, than this incessant business.

Henry David Thoreau (1817–1862), American author and naturalist

Alle thinges obeyen to moneye.

Geoffrey Chaucer (1343–1400), English author

Nothing is more intolerable than a wealthy woman.

Juvenal (60?–130?), Roman lawyer and satirist

Cats of a good breed mouse better when they are fat than when they are starving: and likewise good men who have some talent exercise it to nobler ends when they have wealth enough to live well.

Benvenuto Cellini (1500–1571), Italian sculptor and writer

Nothing is sadder than the consequences of having worldly standards without worldly means.

Van Wyck Brooks (1886–1963), American literary critic

Novel: the man who realizes that one needs to be rich in order to live, who devotes himself completely to the acquisition of money, who succeeds, lives and dies *happy*.

Albert Camus (1913–1960), French existentialist author

Though ye take from a covetous man all his treasure, he has yet one jewel left; ye cannot bereave him of his covetousness.
John Milton (1608–1674), English poet

One has tea out of doors but it's so exquisite. One's cup and saucer gleams and the lemon is new born and nobody *fusses*. That's the chief point of money. One can buy that complete freedom from *fuss*.
Katherine Mansfield (1888–1923), English author

Money is life. Not material life only. It touches the soul. Who steals our purse steals not trash, but our blood, time, muscle, nervous force, our power to help others, our future possibility of turning out creditable work.
Don Marquis (1878–1937), American journalist and humorist

With money I'll throttle the beast-blind world between my fingers. Without it I am strapped; weakened; my life is a curse and a care.
Thomas Wolfe (1900–1938), American novelist

The only people who claim that money is not important are people who have enough money so that they are relieved of the ugly burden of thinking about it.
Joyce Carol Oates (b. 1938), American author

Adversity makes men, and prosperity makes monsters.
Victor Hugo (1802–1885), French author

Don't gamble; take all your savings and buy some good stock and hold it till it goes up, then sell it. If it don't go up, don't buy it.
Will Rogers (1879–1935), American humorist

It isn't necessary to be rich and famous to be happy. It's only necessary to be rich.
Alan Alda (b. 1936), American actor

Money is of value for what it buys, and in love it buys time, place, intimacy, comfort, and a private corner alone.
Mae West (1892–1980), American actor

There is no fire like passion, there is no shark like hatred, there is no snare like folly, there is no torrent like greed.
Buddha (sixth–fifth century B.C.), Indian religious leader

The modern conservative is engaged in one of man's oldest exercises in moral philosophy; that is, the search for a superior moral justification for selfishness.
John Kenneth Galbraith (b. 1908), Canadian-born American economist and educator

Behind every great fortune there is a crime.
Honoré de Balzac (1799–1850), French author

No one can earn a million dollars honestly.
William Jennings Bryan (1860–1925), American political leader

Since I am known as a "rich" person, I feel I have to tip at least $5 each time I check my coat. On top of that, I would have to wear a very expensive coat, and it would have to be insured. Added up, without a topcoat I save over $20,000 a year.
Aristotle Onassis (1900–1975), Greek millionaire ship-builder

Behavior that would be branded as bad taste or bad manners or simply bad by us ordinary mortals becomes a charming idiosyncrasy or eccentricity if one is a genius or has jillions.
Malcolm S. Forbes (1919–1990), American publisher

I believe in inherited wealth. Society needs to have some people who are above it all.
Edward Digby Baltzell, Jr. (b. 1915), American writer and educator

The rich have no need to pronounce their words correctly. They can leave all that to their lawyers and accountants.
Brendan Gill (b. 1914), American critic and author

Form no covetous desire, so that the demon of greediness may not deceive thee, and the treasure of the world may not be tasteless to thee.
Zoroaster (628?–551? B.C.), Persian religious leader

I am not ashamed—because I am not poor; poor are those who crave too many things.
Leonardo da Vinci (1452–1519), Italian painter, sculptor, architect, and engineer

Never economize on luxuries.
Angela Thirkell (1890–1961), English novelist

A large income is the best recipe for happiness I ever heard of.
Jane Austen (1775–1817), English novelist

The question isn't at what age I want to retire, it's at what income.
George Foreman (b. 1948), American boxing champion

Any man who has $10,000 left when he dies is a failure.
Errol Flynn (1909–1959), English-born American actor

The way to make money is to buy when blood is running in the streets.
John D. Rockefeller (1839–1937), American financier

When morality comes up against profit, it is seldom that profit loses.

Shirley Chisholm (b. 1924), American politician and educator

The materialistic idealism that governs American life, that on the one hand makes a chariot of every grocery wagon, and on the other a mere hitching post of every star, lets every man lead a very enticing double life.

Louis Kronenberger (1904–1980), American critic, editor, and author

Our life on earth is, and ought to be, material and carnal. But we have not yet learned to manage our materialism and carnality properly; they are still entangled with the desire for ownership.

E. M. Forster (1879–1970), English novelist

How could there be any question of acquiring or possessing, when the one thing needful for a man is to *become*—to *be* at last, and to die in the fullness of his being.

Antoine de Saint-Exupéry (1900–1944), French author

Accursed greed for gold,
To what doest thou not drive the heart of man?

Virgil (70–19 B.C.), Roman poet

Even genius is tied to profit.

Pindar (518?–?438 B.C.), Greek poet

I finally know what distinguishes man from the other beasts: financial worries.

Jules Renard (1864–1910), French novelist and playwright

The difference between a little money and no money at all is enormous—and can shatter the world. And the difference between a little money and an enormous amount of money is very slight—and that can also shatter the world

Thornton Wilder (1897–1975), American novelist and playwright

I'm living so beyond my income that we may almost be said to be living apart.

e.e. cummings (1894–1962), American poet

The rich will do everything for the poor but get off their backs.

Karl Marx (1818–1883), German philosopher and economist

The trouble with the profit system has always been that is was highly unprofitable to most people.

E. B. White (1899–1985), American author and editor

Money swore an oath that nobody that did not love it should ever have it.

Irish proverb

Everyone lives by selling something.

Robert Louis Stevenson (1850–1894), Scottish novelist and poet

It was left to the present age to endow Covetousness with glamour on a big scale, and to give it a title which it could carry like a flag. It occurred to somebody to call it Enterprise. From the moment of that happy inspiration, Covetousness has gone forward and never looked back.

Dorothy L. Sayers (1893–1957), English writer

Money is not an aphrodisiac: The desire it may kindle in the female eye is more for the cash than the carrier.

Mayra Mannes (1904–1990), American writer

Money may not be your best friend, but it's the quickest to act, and seems to be favorably recognized in more places than most friends are.

Myrtle Reed (1874–1911), American novelist and poet

CHOMP
CHOMP
CHOMP
gluttony

gluttony

Sin: Gluttony

Definition: (glut'-nē), *n.* excessive eating and drinking.

See: edacity; overeating; gourmandism; excess; greed; insatiability; overfeeding; surplus; exorbitance; intoxication; profusion; dissipation; voracity; overloading; immoderation; grossness; feasting; unrestraint; abandon; gorging; luxury; oversupply; selfishness; extravagance; intemperance; debauchery; licentiousness; inebriation; self-indulgence; overabundance; high living; guzzling; piggishness; rapacity; stuffing; gulosity; foodism; good living; polyphagia; belly worship; drunkenness; lavishness

See also: cram; overwhelm; deluge; overstock; devour; inundate; jade; load; consume; swallow; partake; nibble; pick; peck; dine; lunch; sup; make a pig of; eat like a trooper; eat like a horse; eat like a pig; tickle one's palate; lick the plate clean; gulp down; chow down; snap up; fall to; set to; tuck away; tuck into; fork in; spoon in; shovel in; dig in; be a greedy-guts; be an epicure; be a gastronome; be a trencherman; be a bon vivant; be a sensualist; be a bon viveur

See also: **To get** bombed; cockeyed; stupid; leveled; wiped; stewed; totalled; tight; pixilated; addle-pated; blasted; stinko; ripped; schnockered; tanked; soused; looped; wasted; tipsy; loaded; sozzled; blitzed; plastered; blotto; crocked; half-seas over; three sheets to the wind; boozed up; ginned up; liquored up; lit up; flushed; smashed; mellow; in one's cups; roaring drunk; drunk as a skunk; drunk as an owl; drunk as a lord

I always keep a supply of stimulant handy in case I see a snake, which I also keep handy.
W. C. Fields (1879–1946), American comedian

I had left home (like all Jewish girls) in order to eat pork and take birth control pills. When I first shared an intimate evening with my husband, I was swept away by the passion (so dormant inside myself) of a long and tortured existence. The physical cravings I had tried so hard to deny, finally and ultimately sated . . . but enough about the pork.
Roseanne (b. 1953), American comedian and actor

I'm not so think as you drunk I am.
Sir John Squire (1884–1958), English poet and editor

I am as drunk as a lord, but then, I am one, so what does it matter?
Bertrand Russell (1872–1970), English philosopher

Absinthe makes the heart grow fonder.
Esther Watts Mumford (1878–1940), American novelist and playwright

I drink to make other people seem more interesting.
George Jean Nathan (1882–1958), American author and editor

Ernestine Schumann-Heink was a German contralto, noted interpreter of Wagner, and an unabashed gourmand. Enrico Caruso, another lover of good food in quantity, entered the restaurant in which she was dining. Seeing her about to begin on a vast steak, he said, "Stina, surely you are not going to eat that alone."

"No, no, not alone," replied the lady, "Mit potatoes."
As recounted by Clifton Fadiman (b. 1904), American author and editor

I was sitting before my third or fourth Jellybean—which is anisette, grain alcohol, a lit match, and a small wet explosion in the brain.
Louise Erdrich (b. 1954), American writer and poet

Poets have been mysteriously silent on the subject of cheese.
G. K. Chesterton (1874–1936), English journalist and author

[England] is the only country in the world where the food is more dangerous than sex. I mean, a hard cheese will kill you, but a soft cheese will kill you in *seconds*.
Jackie Mason (b. 1931), American comedian and actor

Eating without conversation is only stoking.
Marcelene Cox (twentieth century), American writer

What stops you from killing yourself when you're intoxicated out of your mind is the thought that once you're dead you won't be able to drink any more.
Marguerite Duras (b. 1914), French novelist and filmmaker

We do not desecrate the dish by serving any other, neither salad nor dessert. We just eat Crab Newburg. My friends rise from the table, wring my hand with deep feeling, and slip quietly and reverently away. I sit alone and weep for the misery of a world that does not have blue crabs and a Jersey cow.
Marjorie Kinnan Rawlings (1896–1953), American novelist and journalist

A sudden violent jolt of it has been known to stop the victim's watch, snap his suspenders, and crack his glass eye right across.
Irvin S. Cobb (1876–1944), American author, on moonshine

For two nights the glutton cannot sleep for thinking, first on an empty stomach, and next on a sated stomach.
Shaikh Saadi (1184–1291), Persian poet

Total abstinence is easier for me than perfect moderation.
Saint Augustine (354–430), Christian philosopher

Anyone who tells a lie has not a good heart, and cannot make a good soup.
Ludwig van Beethoven (1770–1827), German composer

A good eater must be a good man; for a good eater must have a good digestion, and a good digestion depends upon a good conscience.
Benjamin Disraeli (1804–1881), English prime minister

When I played drunks I had to remain sober because I didn't know how to play them when I was drunk.
Richard Burton (1925–1984), English actor

The sway of alcohol over mankind is unquestionably due to its power to stimulate the mystical faculties of human nature, usually crushed to earth by the cold facts and dry criticisms of the sober hour. Sobriety diminishes, discriminates, and says no; drunkenness expands, unites, and says yes. Not through mere perversity do men run after it.
William James (1842–1910), American psychologist and philosopher

The cost of living has gone up another quart.
W. C. Fields (1880–1946), American actor

Cherry Cobbler is shortcake with a soul.
Edna Ferber (1887–1968), American writer and playwright

Alcohol flings back, almost illimitably, the boundaries of humor so that we can find uproarious things which our poor sober friends miss altogether. It is necessary, if the joke is really good and really should be shared, to repeat it time and time again until finally it penetrates those solemn skulls.
Jean Stafford (1915–1979), American author

No man is lonely while eating spaghetti.
Frank Morley (1899–1980), English publisher, editor, and writer

I'm on a seafood diet. I see food and I eat it.
Variously ascribed

I've been on a diet for two weeks and all I've lost is two weeks.
Totie Fields (1931–1978), American comedian

No matter what kind of diet you are on, you can usually eat as much as you want of anything you don't like.
Walter Slezak (1902–1983), Austrian-born American actor

The reason fat people are happy is that the nerves are well protected.
Luciano Pavarotti (b. 1935), Italian opera singer

Who ever heard of fat men heading a riot, or herding together in turbulent mobs.
Washington Irving (1783–1859), American author

She could still taste the plump fine oysters that he had ordered for her last meal in the world, the dry sparkle of the vintage Rudesheimer which had cost him the fees of at least five visits to patients, and the ice cream richly sauced with crushed glazed chestnuts which she loved.
Kathryn Hulme (1900–1981), American author

Your truffles must come to the table in their own stock . . . And as you break open this jewel sprung from a poverty-stricken soil, imagine—if you have never visited it—the desolate kingdom where it rules.
Colette (1873–1954), French writer

The truffle is not an outright aphrodisiac, but it may in certain circumstances make women more affectionate and men more amiable.
Anthelme Brillat-Savarin (1755–1826), French politician and author

My grandmother, when she served dinner, was a virtuoso hanging on the edge of her own ecstatic performance . . . She was a little power crazed: She had us and, by God, we were going to eat . . . The futility of saying no was supreme, and no one ever tried it. How could a son-in-law, already weakened near the point of imbecility by the once, twice, thrice charge to the barricades of pork and mashed potato, be expected to gather his feeble wit long enough to ignore the final call of his old commander when she sounded the alarm: "Pie, Fred?"
Patricia Hampl (b. 1946), American writer

To lift off the cover of a tomato-y mixture and let it bubble up mushroom and basil under my nose does a lot to counteract the many subtle efforts a part of me makes to punish myself for all those worst of my shortcomings—those I can neither name nor find a shape for. Terrible brown ghosts with sinews like bedsprings.
Mary Virginia Micka (b. 1922), American poet, educator, activist

An omelette so light we had to lay our knives across it and even then it struggled.
Margaret Halsey (b. 1910), American writer

Roast Beef, Medium, is not only a food. It is a philosophy.
Edna Ferber (1887–1968), American author

Pistachio nuts, the red ones, cure any problem.
Paula Danziger (b. 1944), American writer

Reminds me of my safari in Africa. Somebody forgot the corkscrew and for several days we had to live on nothing but food and water.
W. C. Fields (1880–1946), American comedian

Seeing isn't believing, it's eating that's believing.
James Thurber (1894–1961), American artist and author

There is nothing wrong with sobriety in moderation.
John Ciardi (1916–1986), American poet, critic, and translator

Never eat more than you can lift.
Miss Piggy (Muppets character)

There is no such thing as bad whiskey. Some whiskeys just happen to be better than others. But a man shouldn't fool with booze until he's fifty; then he's a damn fool if he doesn't.
William Faulkner (1897–1962), American novelist

Don't you drink? I notice you speak slightingly of the bottle. I have drunk since I was fifteen and few things have given me more pleasure. When you work hard all day with your head and know you must work again the next day what else can change your ideas and make them run on a different plane like whiskey? When you are cold and wet what else can warm you? Before an attack who can say anything that gives you the momentary well-being that rum does?. . .The only time it isn't good for you is when you write or when you fight. You have to do that cold. But it always helps my shooting. Modern life, too, is often a mechanical oppression and liquor is the only mechanical relief.

Ernest Hemingway (1899–1961), American author

I doubt whether the world holds for any one a more soul-stirring surprise than the first adventure with ice-cream.

Heywood Broun (1888–1939), American journalist and author

Cut out those intimate little dinners for two—unless there's someone with you.

Joey Adams (b. 1911), American comedian

Most British statesmen have either drunk too much or womanised too much. I never fell into the second category.

Lord George-Brown (1914–1985), English statesman

Statistics show that of those who contract the habit of eating, very few survive.

Wallace Irwin (1875–1959), American journalist and author

Like a camel, I can go without a drink for seven days—and have on several horrible occasions.

Herb Caen (b. 1916), American columnist and author

I drink no more than a sponge.

François Rabelais (1490–1553), French humorist and satirist

Boozing does not necessarily have to go hand in hand with being a writer. . . . I therefore solemnly declare to all young men trying to be writers that they do not actually have to become drunkards first.

James Jones (1921–1977), American novelist

Alcohol is the anesthesia by which we endure the operation of life.

George Bernard Shaw (1856–1950), Irish playwright, author, and critic

For a bad hangover, take the juice of two quarts of whiskey.
Eddie Condon (1904–1973), American band leader and musician

The worst thing about some men is that when they are not drunk they are sober.
William Butler Yeats (1865–1939), Irish poet and playwright

There is something in the red of a raspberry pie that looks as good to a man as the red in a sheep looks to a wolf.
Edgar Watson Howe (1853–1937), American editor and author

A fruit is a vegetable with looks and money. Plus, if you let fruit rot, it turns into wine, something Brussels sprouts never do.
P. J. O'Rourke (b. 1947), American humorist

God made only water, but man made wine.
Victor Hugo (1802–1885), French author

In wine there is truth.
Pliny the Elder (23–79), Roman scholar

Only a rank degenerate would drive 1,500 miles across Texas without eating a chicken fried steak.
Larry McMurtry (b. 1936), American novelist

This was a good dinner enough, to be sure; but it was not a dinner to *ask* a man to.
Samuel Johnson (1709–1784), English author

Yes, I was relieved to find that there were still some pigeons left in the squares of San Francisco; it had occurred to me that since my previous visit, every last one of them might have been snatched up, smoked, and thrown on a bed of radicchio.
Calvin Trillin (b. 1935), American journalist and author

What does drunkenness not accomplish? It unlocks secrets, confirms our hopes, urges the indolent into battle, lifts the burden from anxious minds, teaches new arts.
Horace (65–68 B.C.), Roman lyric poet and satirist

I believe, if we take habitual drunkards as a class, their heads and hearts will bear an advantageous comparison to those of any other class. There seems ever to have been a proneness in the brilliant and warm-blooded to fall into this vice.
Abraham Lincoln (1809–1865), sixteenth American president

It is the unbroken testimony of all history that alcoholic liquors have been used by the strongest, wisest, handsomest, and in every way best races of all time.
George Saintsbury (1845–1933), English critic, journalist, and educator

Clearly, some time ago makers and consumers of American junk food passed jointly through some kind of sensibility barrier in the endless quest for new taste sensations. Now they are a little like those desperate junkies who have tried every known drug and are finally reduced to mainlining toilet bowl cleanser in an effort to get still higher.
Bill Bryson (b. 1951), American author and journalist

A good gulp of hot whiskey at bedtime—it's not very scientific, but it helps.
Sir Alexander Fleming (1881–1955), English bacteriologist, inventor of penicillin

A woman should never be seen eating or drinking, unless it be lobster salad and Champagne, the only true feminine & becoming viands.
Lord Byron (1788–1824), English poet

Women alone always order sole. It means something.
John Dos Passos (1896–1970), American novelist

Let the stoics say what they please, we do not eat for the good of living, but because the meat is savory and the appetite is keen.
Ralph Waldo Emerson (1803–1882), American essayist and poet

It's better that it should make you sick than that you don't eat it at all.
Catalan proverb

A man hath no better thing under the sun, than to eat, and to drink, and to be merry.
The Old Testament, Ecclesiastes 8:15

A man who exposes himself when he is intoxicated has not the art of getting drunk.
Samuel Johnson (1709–1784), English author

A meal without flesh is like feeding on grass.
Indian proverb

I drink for the thirst to come.
François Rabelais (1490–1553), French humorist and satirist

There are two reasons for drinking; one is, when you are thirsty, to cure it; the other, when you are not thirsty, to prevent it . . . prevention is better than cure.
Thomas Love Peacock (1785–1866), English novelist and poet

You are not drunk if you can lie on the floor without holding on.
Dean Martin (1917–1996), American singer and actor

It was my uncle George who discovered that alcohol was a food well in advance of modern medicinal thought.
James Thurber (1894–1961), American artist and author

I have often seen the King consume four plates of different soups, a whole pheasant, a partridge, a large plate of salad, two big slices of ham, a dish of mutton in garlic sauce, a plateful of pastries followed by fruit and hard-boiled eggs. The King and Monsieur greatly like hard-boiled eggs.
Duchess of Orléans (1652–1722), sister-in-law of King Louis XIV of France

Drink no longer water, but use a little wine for thy stomach's sake and thine often infirmities.
The New Testament, 1 Timothy 5:23

The Germans are the worst, for sheer bulk. What miles of liver sausage, what oceans of beer and quagmires of those colossal bellies! How appalling they look from behind; the terrible creases of fat three deep across solid and shaven napes. Necks wreathed in smiles, the stigmata of damnation; and delusive smiles, for when they turn around there is nothing but a blank stare and a jigsaw of fencing scars. If you are ever losing an argument with such a one you can always win by telling him to wipe those smiles off the back of his neck.
Patrick Leigh-Fermor (twentieth century), English writer

Alcohol is like love: The first kiss is magic, the second intimate, the third is routine. After that you just take the girl's clothes off.
Raymond Chandler (1888–1959), American author

I must point out that my rule of life is prescribed as an absolutely sacred rite; smoking cigars and also the drinking of alcohol before, after, and if need be, during meals and in the intervals between them.
Sir Winston Churchill (1874–1965), English prime minister and author

Don't eat too many almonds; they add weight to the breasts.

Colette (1873–1954), French writer

To eat well in England you should have breakfast three times a day.

W. Somerset Maugham (1874–1965), English novelist and playwright

You can't drown yourself in drink. I've tried: You float.

John Barrymore (1882–1942), American actor

. . . belching from daily excess, he came hiccupping to the war.

William of Malmesbury (1080–1143), English monk and historian, referring to Philip I of France

Better belly burst than good liquor be lost.

Jonathan Swift (1667–1745), Anglo-Irish author

The advantages of whiskey over dogs are legion. Whiskey does not need to be periodically wormed, it does not need to be fed, it never requires a special kennel, it has no toenails to be clipped or coat to be stripped. Whiskey sits quietly in its special nook until you want it. True, whiskey has a nasty habit of running out, but then so does a dog.

W. C. Fields (1880–1946), American comedian

I'm a man more dined against than dining.

Sir Maurice Bowra (1898–1971), English educator and critic

One drink is too many for me and a thousand not enough.

Brendan Behan (1923–1964), Irish playwright

Outside every fat man there is an even fatter man trying to close in.

Kingsley Amis (b. 1922), English novelist, poet, and critic

Imprisoned in every fat man a thin one is wildly signalling to be let out.

Cyril Connolly (1903–1974), English critic, novelist and editor

Enclosing every thin man, there's a fat man demanding elbow-room.

Evelyn Waugh (1903–1966), English author

Malt does more than Milton can
To justify God's ways to man.

A. E. Housman (1859–1936), English poet and classical scholar

The Right Hon. was a tubby little chap who looked as if he had been poured into his clothes and had forgotten to say "When!"

P. G. Wodehouse (1881–1975), English writer and humorist

I am only a beer teetoaller, not a champagne teetotaller.

George Bernard Shaw (1856–1950), Irish playwright, author, and critic

I'd hate to be a teetotaler. Imagine getting up in the morning and knowing that's as good as you're going to feel all day.

Dean Martin (1917–1996), American singer and actor

It takes a good deal of physical courage to ride a horse. This, however, I have. I get it at about forty cents a flask, and take it as required.

Stephen Leacock (1869–1944), English-born Canadian economist and humorist

You needn't tell me that a man who doesn't love oysters and asparagus and good wines has got a soul, or a stomach either. He's simply got the instinct for being unhappy highly developed.

Saki (1870–1916), Scottish writer and wit

To be a gourmet you must start early, as you must begin riding early to be a good horseman. You must live in France, your father must have been a gourmet. Nothing in life must interest you but your stomach.

Ludwig Bemelmans (1898–1962), Austrian-born American children's book illustrator and writer

[Whiskey is] a torchlight procession marching down your throat.

John L. O'Sullivan (1813–1895), American writer

An alcoholic is someone you don't like who drinks as much as you do.

Dylan Thomas (1914–1953), Welsh poet

One sits the whole day at the desk and appetite is standing next to me. "Away with you," I say. But Comrade Appetite does not budge from the spot.

Leonid Brezhnev (1906–1982), Soviet premier

After eating, an epicure gives a thin smile of satisfaction; a gastronome, burping into his napkin, praises the food in a magazine; a gourmet, repressing his burp, criticizes the food in the same magazine; a gourmand belches happily and tells everybody where he ate; a glutton embraces the white porcelain altar, or more plainly, he barfs.

William Safire (b. 1929), American journalist and author

Let's get out of these wet clothes into a dry martini.

Alexander Woollcott (1887–1943), American journalist (also attributed to others)

Apart from cheese and tulips, the main product of the country [Holland] is advocaat, a drink made from lawyers.
Alan Coren (b. 1938), English writer and journalist

Beer is the Danish national drink, and the Danish national weakness is another beer.
Clementine Paddleford (1900–1967), American journalist and editor

Who could have foretold, from the structure of the brain, that wine could derange its functions.
Hippocrates (460?–377? B.C.), Greek physician

Some people tell you should not drink claret after strawberries. They are wrong.
William Maginn (1794–1842), Irish writer

Now I like claret . . . For really 'tis so fine—it fills one's mouth with a gushing freshness—then goes down cool and feverless . . . and lies as quiet as it did in the grape; then, it is as fragrant as the Queen Bee, and the more ethereal part of it mounts into the brain—not assaulting the cerebral apartments like a bully in a bad-house . . . but rather walks like Aladdin about his own enchanted palace so gently that you do not feel his step.
John Keats (1795–1821), English poet

One cannot think well, love well, sleep well, if one has not dined well.
Virginia Woolf (1882–1941), English author

I hadn't the heart to touch breakfast. I told Jeeves to drink it himself.
P. G. Wodehouse (1881–1975), English writer and humorist

The decline of the aperitif may well be one of the most depressing phenomena of our time.
Luis Buñuel (1900–1983), Spanish filmmaker

No other human being, no woman, no poem or music, book or painting can replace alcohol in its power to give man the illusion of real creation.
Marguerite Duras (b. 1914), French novelist and filmmaker

No power on earth or above the bottomless pit has such influence to terrorize and make cowards of men as the liquor power. Satan could not have fallen on a more potent instrument with which to thrall the world. Alcohol is king!
Eliza "Mother" Stewart (1816–1908), American temperance leader

Even if a cook were to cook a fly, he would keep the breast for himself.
Polish proverb

When I do come to town, bang go my plans in a horrid alcohol explosion that scatters all my good intentions like bits of limbs and clothes over the doorsteps and into the saloon bars of the tawdriest pubs in London.
Dylan Thomas (1914–1953), Welsh poet

I don't drink; I don't like it—it makes me feel good.
Oscar Levant (1906–1972), American humorist and actor

Alcohol is nicissary f'r a man so that now an' thin he can have a good opinion iv himself, ondisturbed be th' facts.
Finley Peter Dunne (1867–1936), American humorist

A gourmet who thinks of calories is like a tart who looks at her watch.
James Beard (1903–1985), American chef and cookbook author

I decided to stop drinking with creeps.
I decided to drink only with friends.
I've lost 30 pounds.
Ernest Hemingway (1899–1961), American author

Fishing, with me, has always been an excuse to drink in the daytime.
Jimmy Cannon (b. 1909), American columnist

Remember, I have taken more out of alcohol than alcohol has taken out of me.
Sir Winston Churchill (1874–1965), English prime minister and author

If you have formed the habit of checking on every new diet that comes along, you will find that, mercifully, they all blur together, leaving you with only one definite piece of information—french fried potatoes are out.
Jean Kerr (b. 1923), American author and playwright

This is one excellent Martini—sort of tastes like it isn't there at all, just a cold cloud.
Herman Wouk (b. 1915), American novelist

When you stop drinking, you have to start dealing with this marvelous personality that started you drinking in the first place.
Jimmy Breslin (b. 1930), American journalist and author

Large, naked, raw carrots are acceptable as food only to those who live in hutches eagerly awaiting Easter.
Fran Liebowitz (b. 1950), American writer

Gluttony is not a secret vice.
Orson Welles (1915–1985), American actor, writer, director, and producer

Wonderful, varied words. Blitzed, blasted, blotto, bombed, cockeyed, crocked, ripped, looped, loaded, leveled, wasted, wiped, soused, sozzled, smashed and schnockered. Stewed, stinko, stupid, tanked, totaled, tight and tipsy. Not to mention feeling no pain, three sheets to the wind, in one's cups, intoxicated, addle-pated and pixilated.
Bruce Weber (b. 1942), American writer

Intemperate temperance injures the cause of temperance, while temperant temperance helps it in its fight against intemperate intemperance.
Mark Twain (1835–1910), American humorist

Vegetarians have wicked, shifty eyes and laugh in a cold, calculating manner. They pinch little children, steal stamps, drink water, favor beards.
J. B. Morton (1893–1979), English writer

I'm not a vegetarian because I love animals; I'm a vegetarian because I hate plants.
A. Whitney Brown (1886–1948), English aviator

Health food may be good for the conscience but Oreos taste a hell of a lot better.
Robert Redford (b. 1937), American actor

Too much and too little wine. Give him none, he cannot find truth; give him too much, the same.
Blaise Pascal (1623–1666), English novelist and poet

Champagne, if you are seeking the truth, is better than a lie detector. It encourages a man to be expansive, even reckless, while lie detectors are only a challenge to tell lies successfully.
Graham Greene (1904–1991), English author

O God, that men should put an enemy in their mouths to steal away their brains! that we should with joy, pleasance, revel, and applause transform ourselves into beasts!
William Shakespeare (1564–1616), English playwright and poet

My whole life revolves around dessert.
Marvin Hamlisch (b. 1944), American composer and musician

I never forget what I eat! I still remember what Marlon [Brando] served me on our first date: cold cauliflower salad and cheap bourbon.
Shelley Winters (b. 1922), American actor

For a bad night, a mattress of wine.
Spanish proverb

A drinking man's someone who wants to forget he isn't still young and believing.
Tennessee Williams (1911–1983), American playwright

[A glutton is] one who takes the piece of pastry you wanted
Anonymous

Gluttony is an emotional escape, a sign that something is eating us.
Peter De Vries (1910–1993), American author

When I behold a fashionable table set out in all its magnificence, I fancy that I see gouts and dropsies, fevers and lethargies, with other innumerable distempers, lying in ambuscade among the dishes. Nature delights in the most plain and simple diet. Herbs are the food of this species, fish of that, and flesh of a third. Man falls upon everything that comes in his way; not the smallest fruit or excrescence of the earth, scarce a berry or a mushroom can escape him.
Joseph Addison (1672–1719), English essayist

Lechery, sir, it [drink] provokes, and unprovokes; it provokes the desire, but it takes away the performance.
William Shakespeare (1564–1616), English playwright and poet

Strange to see how a good dinner and feasting reconciles everybody.
Samuel Pepys (1633–1703), English politician (best known for his *Diary*)

There is nothing to which men, while they have food and drink, cannot reconcile themselves.
George Santayana (1863–1952), Spanish-born American poet and philosopher

Nothing ever tasted better than a cold beer on a beautiful afternoon with nothing to look forward to but more of the same.
Hugh Hood (b. 1928), Canadian novelist

We had gone out there to pass the beautiful day of high summer like true Irishmen—locked in the dark Snug of a public house.
Brendan Behan (1923–1964), Irish playwright

Drinking makes fools of people, and, people are such fools to begin with that it's compounding a felony.
Robert Benchley (1889–1945), American humorist

I believe that if I ever had to practice cannibalism, I might manage it if there were enough tarragon around.
James Beard (1903–1985), American chef and cookbook author

There are more old drunkards than old physicians.

François Rabelais (1490–1553), French humorist and satirist

Boys should abstain from all use of wine until their eighteenth year, for it is wrong to add fire to fire.

Plato (429–347 B.C.), Greek philosopher

The whole world is about three drinks behind.

Humphrey Bogart (1899–1957), American film actor

I like white trash cooking. Cheeseburgers. The greasier the better. Mashed potatoes served in a scoop, a little dent in the top for the gravy. Drake's Devil Dogs for dessert. Pure pleasure; no known nutrient.

Orson Bean (b. 1928), American actor and comedian

I've never been a fan of personality-conflict burgers and identity-crisis omelets with patchouli oil. I function very well on a diet that consists of Chicken Catastrophe and Eggs Overwhelming and a tall, cool Janitor-in-a-Drum. I like to walk out of a restaurant with enough gas to open a Mobil station.

Tom Waits (b. 1949), American singer and songwriter

I've been on a constant diet for the last two decades. I've lost a total of 789 pounds. By all accounts, I should be hanging from a charm bracelet.

Erma Bombeck (1927–1996), American writer and humorist

We frequently hear of people dying from too much drinking. That this happens is a matter of record. But the blame almost always is placed on whisky. Why this should be I never could understand. You can die from drinking too much of anything—coffee, water, milk, soft drinks and all such stuff as that. And so long as the presence of death lurks with anyone who goes through the simple act of swallowing, I will make mine whisky.

W. C. Fields (1880–1946), American comedian

Come quickly, I am tasting stars!

Dom Perignon (1638–1715), at the discovery of champagne

I've never been drunk, but I've often been overserved.

George Gobel (1919–1991), American comedian

I'm scared to death of being stone cold sober.

Jerry Lee Lewis (b. 1935), American rock and country singer

Favorite animal: steak.

Fran Liebowitz (b. 1950), American writer

Fancy cream puffs so soon after breakfast. The very idea made one shudder. All the same, two minutes later Jose and Laura were licking their fingers with the absorbed inward look that only comes from whipped cream.

Katherine Mansfield (1888–1923), English author

Actually, it only takes one drink to get me loaded. Trouble is, I can't remember if it's the thirteenth or fourteenth.

George Burns (1896–1996), American comedian and actor

I think a man ought to get drunk at least twice a year just on principle, so he won't let himself get snotty about it.

Raymond Chandler (1888–1959), American author

I have enough fruitcakes in my freezer to enlarge my patio.

Erma Bombeck (1927–1996), American writer and humorist

I'm no alcoholic. I'm a drunkard. The difference is, drunkards don't go to meetings.

Jackie Gleason (1916–1987), American comedian and actor

Drink always rubbed him the right way.

O. Henry (1862–1910), American short-story writer

The warm, champagny, old-particular, brandy-punchy feeling.

Oliver Wendell Holmes (1941–1935), American jurist

You first parents of the human race. . .who ruined yourself for an apple, what might you not have done for a truffled turkey?

Anthelme Brillat-Savarin (1755–1836), French politician and author

Wine leads to folly. It makes even the wisest laugh too much. It makes him dance. It makes him say what should have been left unsaid.

Homer (850?–800? B.C.), Greek epic poet

When men drink wine they are rich, they are busy, they push lawsuits, they are happy, they help their friends.

Aristophanes (448?–380? B.C.), Greek comic playwright and poet

Wine brings to light the hidden secrets of the soul, gives being to our hopes, bids the coward fight, drives dull care away, and teaches new means for the accomplishment of our wishes.

Horace (65–68 B.C.), Roman lyric poet and satirist

There is more simplicity in the man who eats caviar on impulse than in the man who eats Grapenuts on principle.
G. K. Chesterton (1874–1936), English journalist and author

The best wine . . . goeth down sweetly, causing the lips of those that are asleep to speak.
The Old Testament, Song of Solomon 7:9

Fish, to taste right, must swim three times—in water, in butter, and in wine.
Polish proverb

When the wine goes in the murder comes out.
The Talmud

Acorns were good enough until bread was invented.
Juvenal (60?–130?), Roman lawyer and satirist

You think I am cruel and gluttonous when I beat my cook for sending in a bad dinner. But if that is too trivial a cause, what other can there be for beating a cook?
Martial (40?–104?), Roman poet

Bring in the bottled lightning, a clean tumbler, and a corkscrew.
Charles Dickens (1812–1870), English novelist

Great eaters and great sleepers are incapable of anything else that is great.
Henry IV (1553–1610), king of France

No poems can please for long or live that are written by water-drinkers.
Horace (65–68 B.C.), Roman lyric poet and satirist

A mind of a calibre of mine cannot derive its nutriment from cows.
George Bernard Shaw (1856–1950), Irish playwright, author, and critic

There are two things that will be believed of any man whatsoever, and one of them is that he has taken to drink.
Booth Tarkington (1869–1946), American novelist

Eating should be done in silence, lest the windpipe open before the gullet, and life be in danger.
The Talmud

The Son of man came eating and drinking, and they say, Behold a man gluttonous, and a winebibber, a friend of publicans and sinners.
The New Testament, Matthew 11:19

Be content to remember that those who can make omelettes properly can do nothing else.
Hilaire Belloc (1870–1953), French-born English author

They speak of my drinking, but never think of my thirst.
Scottish proverb

I have been a success: for sixty years I have eaten, and have avoided being eaten.

Logan Pearsall Smith (1865–1946), American essayist

I liked the taste of beer, its live, white lather, its brass-bright depths, the sudden world through the wet-brown walls of the glass, the tilted rush to the lips and the slow swallowing down to the lapping belly, the salt on the tongue, the foam at the corners.

Dylan Thomas (1914–1953), Welsh poet

I am prepared to believe that a dry martini slightly impairs the palate, but think what it does for the soul.

Alec Waugh (1898–1981), English novelist and travel writer

Somewhere lives a bad Cajun cook, just as somewhere must live one last ivory-billed woodpecker. For me, I don't expect ever to encounter either one.

William Least Heat-Moon (b. 1939), American author

Their [the waiters'] eyes sparkled and their pencils flew as she proceeded to eviscerate my wallet—pâté, Whitstable oysters, a sole, filet mignon, and a favorite salad of the Nizam of Hyderbad made of shredded five-pound notes.

S. J. Perelman (1904–1979), American humorist

The Chanukah buckwheat cake or *latke* is much thicker and smaller [than the pancake served in American restaurants] and does not deserve its name unless, when served, it is fairly dripping with fat. It would be futile to attempt a description of it here, for the glories of a successful Chanukah *latke* defy the resources of the richest of Gentile languages.

Abraham Cahan (1860–1951), American journalist and author

Talk of joy: There may be things better than beef stew and baked potatoes and home-made bread—there may be.

David Grayson (1870–1946), American journalist and author

A cup of coffee—real coffee—home-browned, home-ground, home-made, that comes to you dark as a hazel-eye, but changes to a golden bronze as you temper it with cream that never cheated, but was real cream from its birth, thick, tenderly yellow, perfectly sweet, neither lumpy nor frothing on the Java: such a cup of coffee is a match for twenty blue devils, and will exorcise them all.

Henry Ward Beecher (1813–1887), American congregational clergyman

Vienna Coffee! That sumptuous coffee-house coffee, compared with which all other European and all American hotel coffee is mere fluid poverty.

Mark Twain (1835–1910), American humorist

Talking of Pleasure, this moment I was writing with one hand and with the other holding to my Mouth a Nectarine—good God how fine. It went down soft, pulpy, slushy, oozy—all its delicious embodiment melted down my throat like a large Beautiful, strawberry . . . .

John Keats (1795–1821), English poet

Coleridge holds that a man cannot have a pure mind who refuses apple dumplings, I am not certain but he is right.

Charles Lamb (1775–1834), English essayist and critic

What I say is that, if a man really likes potatoes, he must be a pretty decent sort of fellow.

A. A. Milne (1882–1956), English writer

Gimme four steaks, a dozen eggs, pound of bacon, three kegs of beer, fifteen potatoes, eighteen whores, seven cigars, and a dish of chocolate ice cream.

Babe Ruth (1895–1948), American baseball player, ordering dinner

Ask not what you can do for your country. Ask what's for lunch.

Orson Welles (1915–1985), American actor, writer, director, and producer

Mr. Leopold Bloom ate with relish the inner organs of beasts and fowls. He liked thick giblet soup, nutty gizzards, a stuffed roast heart, liverslices fried with crustcrumbs, fried hencod's roes. Most of all he liked grilled mutton kidneys which gave to his palate a fine tang of faintly scented urine.

James Joyce (1882–1941), Irish novelist, poet, and playwright

I bought buckets of caviar and asked all the greediest people I know. They sat in a holy circle and never spoke to me once, except to say, in loud asides, that the others were making pigs of themselves.

Nancy Mitford (1904–1974), English author

He that but looketh on a plate of ham and eggs to lust after it, hath already committed breakfast with it in his heart.

C. S. Lewis (1898–1963), English literary scholar

I see no objection to stoutness, in moderation.

W. S. Gilbert (1836–1911), English librettist

Since I saw you I have been in France, and have eaten frogs. The nicest little rabbity things you ever tasted. Do look about for them. Make Mrs. Clare pick off the hind quarters, boil them plain, with parsley and butter. The fore quarters are not so good. She may let them hop off by themselves.
Charles Lamb (1775–1834), English essayist and critic

God forgives the sin of gluttony.
Catalan proverb

Great restaurants are, of course, nothing but mouth-brothels. There is no point in going to them if one intends to keep one's belt buckled.
Raphael (1483–1520), Italian painter

He who distinguishes the true savor of his food can never be a glutton; he who does not cannot be otherwise.
Henry David Thoreau (1817–1862), American author and naturalist

sloth

sloth

Sin: Sloth

Definition: Sloth (slôth), *n.* habitual disinclination to exertion.

See: idleness; languor; laziness; apathy; indolence; lethargy; torpor; listlessness; passivity; sluggishness; inattention; nonchalance; lassitude; insensibility; procrastination; deferral; acedia; lallygagging; goldbricking; shirking; malingering; shillyshallying; shiftlessness; fainéance; quiescence; stillness; quietness; immobility; inaction; cessation; dullness; inertia; indolence; indifference; inertness; otiosity; nonactivity; unarousedness; unexcitability; lifelessness; inanimation; negligence; supineness; dilatoriness; dissipation; dissoluteness

See also: delay; stall; postpone; lag; wait; dawdle; linger; drag; poke; dally; stagnate; vegetate; loaf; cadge; sponge;

lounge; mooch; drift; stop; cease; rest; tarry; relax; coast; halt; loll; decelerate; check; brake; loiter; play; pull up; kill time; come to a stand still; remain at anchor; hang around; while away the time; dabble in; have a break; take one's pleasure; goof off; slow down; lie around; do nothing; hold up; lie fallow; be stuporous; be a slug-a-bed; be impassive; be sedentary; be phlegmatic; be dormant; be chair-borne; be stolid; be at leisure; be a couch potato; be remiss; be unproductive; be lumpish; be disinterested

Aerobics must be the least appealing activity, I don't even know how this word came into being: *aerobics*. I guess gym instructors got together and said, "If we're going to charge ten dollars an hour, we can't call it 'jumping up and down.'"
Rita Rudner (b. 1955), American comedian and actor

The word *aerobics* comes from two Greek words: *aero*, meaning "ability to," and *bics*, meaning "withstand tremendous boredom."
Dave Barry (b. 1948), American humorist

If it were not for the demands made upon me by my business, I would provide living proof that a man can live quite happily for decades without doing any work.
J. Paul Getty (1892–1976), American oil magnate

You must have been warned against letting the golden hours slip by. Yes, but some of them are golden only because we let them slip.
J. M. Barrie (1860–1937), Scottish novelist and playwright

The only reason I would take up jogging is to hear heavy breathing again.
Erma Bombeck (1927–1996), American writer and humorist

When I feel like exercising I just lie down until the feeling goes away.
Chancey Depew (1834–1928), American lawyer and businessman

Exercise is the most awful illusion. The secret is a lot of aspirin and marron glacés.
Noël Coward (1899–1973), English actor and playwright

The word *Sloth* is seldom on modern lips. When used, it is a mildly facetious variant of "indolence," and indolence, surely, so far from being a deadly sin, is one of the most amiable of weaknesses. Most of the world's troubles seem to come from people who are too busy. If only politicians and insects were lazier, how much happier we should all be. The lazy man is preserved from the commission of almost all the nastier crimes, and many of the motives which make us sacrifice to toil the innocent enjoyment of leisure, are among the most ignoble—pride, avarice, emulation, vainglory and the appetite for power over others.
Evelyn Waugh (1903–1966), English author

Never do today what you can do as well tomorrow.
Aaron Burr (1756–1836), American Revolutionary officer and politician

Never put off until tomorrow what you can do the day after tomorrow.
Mark Twain (1835–1910), American humorist

Idleness is fatal only to the mediocre.
Albert Camus (1913–1960), French author and existentialist

I swear they are all beautiful, everyone that sleeps is beautiful.
Walt Whitman (1819–1892), American poet

A sleeping person induces respect, almost as much as a dead one. So that even the Greek gods, when they eavesdropped on naked girls asleep, dared at the most, a kiss.
Emil Ludwig (1881–1948), German biographer

Lying in bed would be an altogether perfect and supreme experience if only one had a coloured pencil long enough to draw on the ceiling.
G. K. Chesterton (1874–1936), English journalist and author

The horror of getting up is unparalled, and I am filled with amazement every morning when I find that I have done it.
Lytton Strachey (1880–1932), English biographer and historian

Sleep faster, we need the pillows.
Yiddish proverb

Loafing needs no explanation and is its own excuse.
Christopher Morley (1890–1957), American author

A good rest is half the work.
Yugoslav proverb

The reason American cities are prosperous is that there is no place to sit down.
Alfred J. Talley (1877–1952), American jurist

Some are born lazy, some have idleness thrust upon them and others spend a great deal of effort creating a careless nonchalance.
Beryl Downing (twentieth century), English journalist

Work is the only dirty four-letter word in the language.
Abbie Hoffman (1936–1989), American political activist and author

My sole literary ambition is to write one good novel, then retire to my hut in the desert, assume the lotus position, compose my mind and senses, and sink into meditation, contemplating my novel.
Edward Abbey (1927–1989), American writer

Anybody who works is a fool. I don't work, I merely inflict myself on the public.
Robert Morley (1908–1992), American actor and playwright

Work is the curse of the drinking class.
Mike Romanoff (1890–1971), American restaurateur

How beautiful it is to do nothing, and then rest afterward.
Spanish proverb

Most Americans are born drunk, and really require a little wine or beer to sober them. They have a sort of permanent intoxication from within, a sort of invisible champagne . . . Americans do not need to drink to inspire them to do anything, although they do sometimes, I think, need a little for the deeper and more delicate purpose of teaching them how to do nothing.
G. K. Chesterton (1874–1936), English journalist and author

[Leisure is] the best of all possessions.
Socrates (469–399 B.C.), Greek philosopher

The world is full of willing people. Some willing to work, the rest willing to let them.
Robert Frost (1874–1963), American poet

When God foreclosed on Eden, he condemned Adam and Eve to go to work. Work has never recovered from the humiliation.
Lance Morrow (b. 1939), American journalist and author

They say hard work never hurt anybody, but I figure why take the chance.
Ronald Reagan (b. 1911), American actor and fortieth president

Anyone can do any amount of work, provided it isn't the work he's supposed to be doing.
Robert Benchley (1889–1945), American humorist

It is impossible to enjoy idling thoroughly unless one has plenty of work to do. There is no fun in doing nothing when you have nothing to do. Wasting time is merely an occupation then, and a most exhausting one. Idleness, like kisses, to be sweet must be stolen.
Jerome K. Jerome (1859–1927), English humorist, novelist, and playwright

Any fool can be fussy and rid himself of energy all over the place, but a man has to have something in him before he can settle down to nothing.
J. B. Priestley (1894–1984), English novelist, critic, and playwright

Do nothing in particular, and do it very well.
W. S. Gilbert (1836–1911), English librettist

There are only the pursued, the pursuing, the busy, and the tired.
F. Scott Fitzgerald (1896–1940), American author

It is better to have loafed and lost than never to have loafed at all.

James Thurber (1894–1961), American artist and author

Three o'clock is always too late or too early for anything you want to do.

Jean-Paul Sartre (1905–1980), French existentialist author

I am happiest when I am idle. I could live for months without performing any kind of labor, and at the expiration of that time I should feel fresh and vigorous enough to go right on in the same way for numerous more months.

Artemus Ward (1834–1867), American humorist

I made up my mind long ago that life was too short to do anything for myself that I could pay others to do for me.

W. Somerset Maugham (1874–1965), English novelist and playwright

Everyone confesses in the abstract that exertion which brings out all the powers of body and mind is the best thing for us all; but practically most people do all they can to get rid of it, and as a general rule nobody does much more than circumstances drive them to.

Harriet Beecher Stowe (1811–1896), American author

Alas, the flesh is weary, and I've read all the books.

Stéphane Mallarmé (1842–1898), French poet

I do not care for anything. I do not care to ride, for the exercise is too violent. I do not care to walk, walking is to strenuous. I do not care to lie down, for I should either have to remain lying, and I do not care to do that, or I should have to get up again, and I do not care to do that either. *Summa summarum*: I do not care at all.

Søren Kierkegaard (1813–1855), Danish philosopher and theologian

Idleness is an appendix to nobility.

Robert Burton (1577–1640), English clergyman and author

It is a fact that not once in all my life have I gone out for a walk. I have been taken out for walks; but that is another matter.

Max Beerbohm (1872–1956), English critic and caricaturist

The man who does not betake himself at once and desperately to sawing is called a loafer, though he may be knocking at the doors of heaven all the while.

Henry David Thoreau (1817–1862), American author and naturalist

Yet it is in our idleness, in our dreams, that the submerged truth sometimes comes to the top.

Virginia Woolf (1882–1941), English author

I have long been of the opinion that if work were such a splendid thing the rich would have kept more of it for themselves.

Bruce Grocott (b. 1940), English labor politician

Prostration is our natural position. A wormlike movement from a spot of sunlight to a spot of shade, and back, is the type of movement that is natural to men.

Wyndham Lewis (1882–1957), English novelist, essayist, and painter

Industrial man—a sentient reciprocating engine having a fluctuating output, coupled to an iron wheel revolving with uniform velocity. And then we wonder why this should be the golden age of revolution and mental derangement.

Aldous Huxley (1894–1963), English author

Personally, I have nothing against work, particularly when it is performed, quietly and unobtrusively, by someone else. I just don't happen to think it's an appropriate subject of a "ethic."

Barbara Ehrenreich (b. 1941), American sociologist and feminist

It is already possible to imagine a society in which the majority of the population, that is to say, its laborers, will have almost as much leisure as in earlier times was enjoyed by the aristocracy. When one recalls how aristocracies in the past actually behaved, the prospect is not cheerful.

W. H. Auden (1907–1973), English poet

We owe most of our great inventions and most of the achievements of genius to idleness—either enforced or voluntary. The human mind prefers to be spoon-fed with the thoughts of others, but deprived of such nourishment it will, reluctantly, begin to think for itself—and such thinking, remember, is original thinking and may have valuable results.

Dame Agatha Christie (1891–1976), English author

Idleness [is] only a coarse name for my infinite capacity for living in the present.

Cyril Connolly (1903–1974), English critic, writer, and editor

Happy is the man with a wife to tell him what to do and a secretary to do it.
Lord Mancroft (1914–1987), English politician

For one person who dreams of making fifty thousand pounds, a hundred people dream of being left fifty thousand pounds.
A. A. Milne (1882–1956), English writer

Give me books, fruit, French wine and fine weather and a little music out of doors, played by somebody I do not know.
John Keats (1795–1821), English poet

Exercise is the yuppie version of bulimia.
Barbara Ehrenreich (b. 1941), American sociologist and feminist

I should have worked just long enough to discover that I didn't like it.
Paul Theroux (b. 1941), American novelist and travel writer

I make no secret of the fact that I would rather lie on a sofa than sweep beneath it. But you have to be efficient if you're going to be lazy.
Shirley Conran (b. 1932), English journalist and designer

The only exercise I get is when I take the studs out of one shirt and put them in another.
Ring Lardner (1885–1933), American humorist and short-story writer

Any discussion of Sloth in the present day is of course incomplete without considering television, with its gifts of paralysis, along with its creature and symbiont, the notorious Couch Potato. Tales spun in idleness find us Tubeside, supine, chiropractic fodder, sucking it all in, reenacting in reverse the transaction between dream and revenue that brought these colored shadows here to begin with so that we might feed, uncritically, committing the six other deadly sins in parallel, eating too much, envying the celebrated, coveting merchandise, lusting after images, angry at the news, perversely proud of whatever distance we may enjoy between our couches and what appears on the screen.
Thomas Pynchon (b. 1937), American novelist

Exercise is bunk. If you are healthy, you don't need it; if you are sick you shouldn't take it.
Henry Ford (1863–1947), American automobile manufacturer

If I had no duties, and no reference to futurity, I would spend my life in driving briskly in a post-chaise with a pretty woman.
Samuel Johnson (1709–1784), English author

One of the symptoms of approaching nervous breakdown is the belief that one's work is terribly important, and that to take a holiday would bring all kinds of disaster. If I were a medical man, I should prescribe a holiday to any patient who considered his work important.
Bertrand Russell (1872–1970), English philosopher

There are men here and there to whom the whole of life is like an after-dinner hour with a cigar; easy, pleasant, empty, perhaps enlivened by some fable of strife to be forgotten—before the end is told—even if there happens to be any end to it.
Joseph Conrad (1857–1924), English novelist

The present generation, wearied by its chimerical efforts, relapses into complete indolence. Its condition is that of a man who has only fallen asleep towards morning: first of all come great dreams, then a feeling of laziness, and finally a witty or clever excuse for remaining in bed.
Søren Kierkegaard (1813–1855), Danish philosopher and theologian

No longer diverted by other emotions, I work the way a cow grazes.
Käthe Kollwitz (1867–1945), German graphic artist and sculptor

You'll never succeed in idealizing hard work. Before you can dig mother earth you've got to take off your ideal jacket. The harder a man works, at brute labor, the thinner becomes his idealism, the darker his mind.
D. H. Lawrence (1885–1930), English novelist

A broad margin of leisure is as beautiful in a man's life as in a book. Haste makes waste, no less in life than in housekeeping. Keep the time, observe the hours of the universe, not of the cars. What are threescore years and ten hurriedly and coarsely lived to moments of divine leisure in which your life is coincident with the life of the universe?
Henry David Thoreau (1817–1862), American author and naturalist

What'll we do with ourselves this afternoon? And the day after that, and the next thirty years.
F. Scott Fitzgerald (1896–1940), American author

People who work sitting down get paid more than people who work standing up.
Ogden Nash (1902–1971), American poet

Work is a form of nervousness.
Don Herold (nineteenth–twentieth century), American author

One of the saddest things is that the only thing that a man can do for eight hours a day, day after day, is work. You can't eat eight hours a day nor drink for eight hours nor make love for eight hours—all you can do for eight hours is work. Which is the reason why man makes himself and everybody else so miserable and unhappy.
William Faulkner (1897–1962), American novelist

My father taught me to work. He did not teach me to love it.
Abraham Lincoln (1809–1865), sixteenth American president

The only athletic sport I ever mastered was backgammon.
Douglas Jerrold (1803–1857), English playwright and humorist

I like long walks, especially when they are taken by people who annoy me.
Fred Allen (1894–1956), American humorist

I am a friend of the workingman, and I would rather be his friend than be one.
Clarence Darrow (1857–1938), American lawyer, lecturer, and writer

Some folks can look so busy doing nothin' that they seem indispensable.
Frank McKinney Hubbard (1868–1930), American caricaturist and humorist

The secret of being truly successful, I believe, is that they learned very early in life how *not* to be busy. They saw through that adage, repeated to me so often in childhood, that anything worth doing is worth doing well. The truth is, many things are worth doing only in the most slovenly, half-hearted fashion possible, and many other things are not worth doing at all.
Barbara Ehrenreich (b. 1941), American sociologist and feminist

The first external revelations of the dry-rot in men is a tendency to lurk and lounge; to be at street corners without intelligible reason; to be going anywhere when met; to be about many places rather than any; to do nothing tangible but to have the intention of performing a number of tangible duties tomorrow or the day after.
Charles Dickens (1812–1870), English novelist

When everybody is occupied, we only speak when we have something to say; but when we are doing nothing, we are compelled to be always talking; and of all torments that is the most annoying and the most dangerous.
Jean-Jacques Rousseau (1712–1778), French philosopher and author

To be idle and to be poor have always been reproaches; and therefore every man endeavors with his utmost care to hide his poverty from others, and his idleness from himself.
Samuel Johnson (1709–1784), English author

Take away leisure and Cupid's bow is broken.
Ovid (43 B.C.–A.D. 17?), Roman poet

But he must know, that in this theater of man's life it is reserved only for God and angels to be lookers on.
Sir Francis Bacon (1561–1626), English philosopher and author

Life is one long process of getting tired.
Samuel Butler (1835–1902), English author

If you are losing your leisure, look out! You may be losing your soul.
Logan Pearsall Smith (1865–1946), American essayist

It is an undoubted truth that the less one has to do the less time one finds to do it in. One yawns, one procrastinates, one can do it when one will, and, therefore, one seldom does it at all; whereas, those who have a great deal of business must buckle to it; and then they always find time enough to do it.
Lord Chesterfield (1694–1773), English statesman

[Laziness] is the habit of resting before fatigue sets in.
Jules Renard (1864–1910), French author

[Leisure] is ease . . . with dignity.
Marcus Tullius Cicero (106–43 B.C.), Roman orator and philosopher

If the world were not so full of people, and most of them did not have to work so hard, there would be more time for them to get out and lie on the grass, and there would be more grass for them to lie on.
Don Marquis (1878–1937), American journalist and humorist

We are always getting ready to live, but never living.
Ralph Waldo Emerson (1803–1882), American essayist and poet

Life, as it is called, is for most of us one long postponement.
Henry Miller (1891–1980), American novelist

Back in the days when unremitting toil was the lot of all but the very few and leisure still a hopeless yearning, hard and painful as life was, it still felt real. People were in rapport with the small bit of reality allotted to them, the sense of the earth, the tang of the changing seasons, the consciousness of the eternal on-going of birth and death. Now, when so many have leisure, they become detached from themselves, not merely from the earth. From all widened horizons of our greater world a thousand voices call us to come near, to understand, and to enjoy, but our ears are not trained to hear them. The leisure is ours but not the skill to use it.
Robert Morrison MacIver (1882–1970), American educator and author

One of these days is none of these days.
English proverb

It is necessary to work, if not from inclination, at least from despair. Everything considered, work is less boring than amusing oneself.
Charles Baudelaire (1821–1867), French poet

Work is not the curse, but drudgery is.
Henry Ward Beecher (1813–1887), American congregational clergyman

The ant is knowing and wise; but he doesn't know enough to take a vacation.
Clarence Day (1874–1935), American author

Where there is most labour there is not always most life.
Havelock Ellis (1859–1939), English scientist and author

The life of labor does not make men, but drudges.
Ralph Waldo Emerson (1803–1882), American essayist and poet

Do your work with your whole heart and you will succeed—there is so little competition!
Elbert Hubbard (1856–1915), American author and editor

A man is not idle because he is absorbed in thought. There is a visible labour and there is an invisible labour.
Victor Hugo (1802–1885), French author

How Sunday into Monday melts!
Ogden Nash (1902–1971), American poet

Death is the end of life; ah, why
Should life all labor be?
Alfred, Lord Tennyson (1809–1892), English poet

Tomorrow is often the busiest day of the year.
Spanish proverb

Any fool can be fussy and rid himself of energy all over the place, but a man has to have something in him before he can settle down to do nothing.

J. B. Priestley (1894–1984), English novelist, critic, and playwright

Of all our faults, the one that we excuse most easily is idleness.

Duc François de la Rochefoucauld (1613–1680), French author

Even if a farmer intends to loaf, he gets up in time to get an early start.

Edgar Watson Howe (1853–1937), American editor and author

I have enough money to get by. I'm not independently wealthy, just independently lazy, I suppose.

Montgomery Clift (1920–1966), American actor

The need of exercise is a modern superstition, invented by people who ate too much, and had nothing to think about. Athletics don't make anybody either long-lived or useful.

George Santayana (1863–1952), Spanish-born American poet and philosopher

The secret of being miserable is to have the leisure to bother about whether you're happy or not.

George Bernard Shaw (1856–1950), Irish playwright, author, and critic

It's unnatural for people to run around city streets unless they are thieves or victims. It makes people nervous to see someone running. I know that when I see someone running on my street my instincts tell me to let the dog out after him.

Mike Royko (1932–1997), American newspaper columnist

That man is idle who can do something better.

Ralph Waldo Emerson (1803–1882), American essayist and poet

[Idleness is] a genius for doing nothing, and doing it assiduously.

Thomas C. Haliburton (1796–1865), Canadian jurist and humorist

Procrastination is the art of keeping up with yesterday.

Don Marquis (1878–1937), American journalist and humorist

Early to rise and early to bed makes a man healthy, wealthy and dead.

James Thurber (1894–1961), American artist and author

Hard work never killed anybody, but why take the chance?

Edgar Bergen (1903–1978), American ventriloquist

So little time, so little to do.

Oscar Levant (twentieth century 1906–1972), American humorist and actor

Hard work is damn near as overrated as monogamy.

Huey P. Long (1893–1935), American politician

The fitness business is about sex and immortality. By toning up the system, you can prolong youth, just about finesse middle age and then, when the time comes, go straight into senility.

Wilfrid Sheed (b. 1930), English-born American novelist and journalist

I don't mind exercise, but it's a private activity. Joggers should run in a wheel—like hamsters—because *I* don't want to look at them. And I really hate people who go on an airplane in jogging outfits. That's a major offense today, even bigger than Spandex bicycle pants. You see eighty-year-old women coming on the plane in jogging outfits for comfort. Well, *my* comfort—my mental comfort—is completely ruined when I see them coming. You're on an airplane, not in your bedroom, so please! And I really hate walkathons. Blocking traffic, people patting themselves on the back. The whole attitude offends me. They have this smug look on their faces as they hold you up in traffic so that they can give two cents to some charity.

John Waters (b. 1946), American film director

I'm Jewish. I don't work out. If God had intended me to bend over, He'd have put diamonds on the floor.

Joan Rivers (b. 1933), American comedian

As a confirmed melancholic, I can testify that the best and maybe only antidote for melancholia is *action*. However, like most melancholics, I suffer also from sloth.

Edward Abbey (1927–1989), American writer

I have no plans. And no plans to plan.

Mario Cuomo (b. 1932), American politician

I am interested in leisure the way a poor man is interested in money. I can't get enough of it.

Prince Philip (b. 1921), husband of Queen Elizabeth II of England

I am not one of those people who would rather act than eat. Quite the reverse. My own desire as a boy was to retire. That ambition has never changed.

George Sanders (1906–1972), American actor

Sloth is the tempter that beguiles, and expels from paradise.

Amos Bronson Alcott (1799–1888), American transcendentalist, teacher, and writer

No man who is in a hurry is quite civilized.

Will Durant (1885–1981), American editor and author

Every once in a while it is important to do nothing . . . . Nothing is harder to do. Some puritan perversity in the American character makes us hate the nothing-doers of the world. A man quietly doing nothing is a challenge to the American system. He must be cajoled, badgered and, if necessary, blackguarded into purposeful living.

Russell Baker (b. 1925), American journalist and author

The more characteristic American hero in the earlier day, and the more beloved type at all times, was not the hustler but the whittler.

Mark Sullivan (1874–1952), American journalist

Wisely and slowly; they stumble that run fast.

William Shakespeare (1564–1616), English playwright and poet

I have all my life long been lying [in bed] till noon; yet I tell all young men, and tell them with great sincerity, that nobody who does not rise early will ever do any good.

Samuel Johnson (1709–1784), English author

He who hesitates is sometimes saved.

James Thurber (1894–1961), American artist and author

It's necessary to be slightly underemployed if you are to do something significant.

James Watson (b. 1928), American geneticist

Leisure should be relaxing. Possibly you like complicated puzzles or chess, or other demanding intellectual games. Give them up. If you want to continue to be intellectually productive, you must risk the contempt of your younger acquaintances and freely admit that you read detective stories or watch Archie Bunker on television.

B. F. Skinner (1904–1990), American psychologist

A loafer always has the correct time.

Frank McKinney Hubbard (1868–1930), American caricaturist and humorist

Not everything that is more difficult is more meritorious.

Saint Thomas Aquinas (1225–1274), Italian Dominican monk and theologian

[Work is] the greatest thing in the world, so we should always save some of it for tomorrow.

Don Herold (nineteenth–twentieth century), American author

I have so much to do that I am going to bed.

Savoyard proverb

Necessity is the constant scourge of the lower classes, ennui of the higher ones.
Arthur Schopenhauer (1788–1860), German philosopher

There are but few men who have character enough to lead lives of idleness.
Henry Wheeler Shaw (1818–1885), American humorist

IDLENESS: *n.* A model farm where the devil experiments with seeds of new sins and promotes the growth of staple vices.
Ambrose Bierce (1842–1914), American writer

There is one piece of advice, in a life of study, which I think no one will object to; and that is, every now and then to be completely idle—to do nothing at all.
Sydney Smith (1771–1845), English clergyman, essayist, and wit

[Procrastination is] hardening of the oughteries.
Anonymous

The occupation most becoming to a civilized man is to do nothing.
Théophile Gautier (1811–1872), French poet and novelist

I am not an actor, I am a spectator only. My sole occupation is sight-seeing. In a certain imperial idleness, I amuse myself with the world.
Alexander Smith (1830–1867), American humorist

I like to rest, whether sitting or lying down, with my heels as high as my head, or higher.
Michel Eyquem de Montaigne (1533–1592), French essayist

Tranquility is the old man's milk. I go to enjoy it in a few days, and to exchange the roar and tumult of bulls and bears for the prattle of my grandchildren and senile rest.
Thomas Jefferson (1743–1826), third American president

That's not exercise, it's flagellation.
Noël Coward (1899–1973), English actor and playwright, in reference to squash

Games played with the ball, and others of that nature are too violent for the body and stamp no character on the mind.
Thomas Jefferson (1743–1826), third American president

The aim of education is the wise use of leisure.
Aristotle (384–322 B.C.), Greek philosopher

They talk of the dignity of work. Bosh—the dignity is in leisure.
Herman Melville (1819–1891), American novelist

As a boy he swallowed a teaspoon. And he hasn't stirred since.
Anonymous

If you can spend a perfectly useless afternoon in a perfectly useless manner, you have learned how to live.
Lin Yutang (1895–1976), Chinese-born American writer

In the name of God, stop a moment, cease your work, look around you . . . .
Leo Tolstoy (1828–1910), Russian novelist, philosopher, and mystic

It takes a lot of time to be a genius, you have to sit around so much doing nothing, really doing nothing.
Gertrude Stein (1874–1946), American author

Sit in reverie, and watch the changing color of the waves that break upon the idle seashore of the mind.
Henry Wadsworth Longfellow (1807–1882), American poet

Never do anything standing that you can do sitting, or anything sitting that you can do lying down.
Chinese proverb

Lost, yesterday, somewhere between sunrise and sunset, two golden hours, each set with sixty diamond minutes. No reward is offered, for they are gone forever.
Horace Mann (1796–1859), American educator

Each day, and the living of it, has to be a conscious creation in which discipline and order are relieved with some play and pure foolishness.
May Sarton (1912–1995), American writer

The most thoroughly wasted of all days is that on which one has not laughed.
Nicholas de Chamfort (1772–1834), French author

We should consider every day lost on which we have not danced at least once.
Friedrich Nietzsche (1844–1900), German philosopher and poet

I finally figured out the only reason to be alive is to enjoy it.
Rita Mae Brown (b. 1944), American writer and playwright

Come, let us give a little time to folly . . . and even in a melancholy day let us find time for an hour of pleasure.
Saint Bonaventura (1221–1274), Italian theologian

Let us live, while we are alive!
Johann Wolfgang von Goethe (1749–1832), German poet and philosopher

I take it as a prime cause of the present confusion of society that it is too sickly and too doubtful to use pleasure as a test of value.
Rebecca West (1892–1983), English critic and novelist

There is no cure for birth and death save to enjoy the interval.
George Santayana (1863–1952), Spanish-born American poet and philosopher

The business of life is to enjoy oneself; everything else is a mockery.
Norman Douglas (1868–1952), English author

The true object of human life is play.
G. K. Chesterton (1874–1936), English journalist and author

Pleasure is the object, duty and the goal of all rational creatures.
Voltaire (1694–1778), French author

Bowmen bend their bows when they wish to shoot; unbrace them when the shooting is over. Were they kept always strung they would break and fail the archer in a time of need. So it is with men. If they give themselves constantly to serious work, and never indulge awhile in pastime or sport, they lose their senses and become mad.
Herodotus (fifth century B.C.), Greek historian

It is related of an Englishman that he hanged himself to avoid the daily task of dressing and undressing.
Johann Wolfgang von Goethe (1749–1832), German poet and philosopher

Mr. [Calvin] Coolidge's genius for inactivity is developed to a very high point. It is far from being an indolent activity. It is a grim, determined, alert inactivity which keeps Mr. Coolidge occupied constantly. Nobody has ever worked harder at inactivity, with such force of character, with such unremitting attention to detail, with such conscientious devotion to the task.
Walter Lippmann (1889–1974), American writer

If you don't want to work, you have to work to earn enough money so that you won't have to work.
Ogden Nash (1902–1971), American poet

Like every man of sense and good feeling, I abominate work.
Aldous Huxley (1894–1963), English author

It takes application, a fine sense of value, and a powerful community-spirit for a people to have serious leisure, and this has not been the genius of the Americans.
Paul Goodman (1911–1992), American author, poet, and critic

There can be no high civilization where there is not ample leisure.

Henry Ward Beecher (1813–1887), American congregational clergyman

To be at ease is better than to be at business. Nothing really belongs to us but time, which even he has who has nothing else.

Baltasar Gracian (1601–1658), Spanish prose writer and Jesuit priest

Without leisure there can be neither art nor science nor fine conversation, nor any ceremonious performance of the offices of love and friendship.

Lewis Mumford (1895–1990), American writer

In itself and in its consequences the life of leisure is beautiful and ennobling in all civilised men's eyes.

Thorstein Veblen (1857–1929), American economist and social philosopher

Delay is preferable to error.

Thomas Jefferson (1743–1826), third American president

[Leisure is] Ease . . . with dignity.

Marcus Tullius Cicero (106–43 B.C.), Roman orator and philosopher

Increased means and increased leisure are the two civilizers of man.

Benjamin Disraeli (1804–1881), English prime minister and author

To be able to fill leisure intelligently is the last product of civilization, and at present very few people have reached this level.

Bertrand Russell (1872–1970), English philosopher

We are great fools. "He has spent his life in idleness," we say; "I have done nothing today." What, have you not lived?

Michel Eyquem de Montaigne (1533–1592), French essayist

A life spent in constant labor is a life wasted, save a man be such a fool as to regard a fulsome obituary notice as an ample reward.

George Jean Nathan (1882–1958), American editor, author, and critic

There is no pleasure in having nothing to do; the fun is in having lots to do—and not doing it.

Mary Wilson Little (nineteenth century), American writer

Certain days set apart by the church to be spent in holy idleness, which is favorable to piety. . . . The safest way of passing such days is to sit and yawn your head off.

Voltaire (1694–1778), French author

I loaf and invite my soul.

Walt Whitman (1819–1892), American poet

The English take their pleasures sadly, after the fashion of their country.

Duc de Sully (1560–1641), French Huguenot soldier, financier, and statesman

The vigorous are no better than the lazy during one half of life, for all men are alike when asleep.

Aristotle (384–322 B.C.), Greek philosopher

Blest be the man who first invented sleep—a cloak to cover all human imaginings, food to satisfy hunger, water to quench thirst, fire to warm cold air, cold to temper heat, and, lastly, a coin to buy whatever we need.

Miguel de Cervantes (1547–1616), Spanish novelist

[Work is] an activity reserved for the dullard. It is the very opposite of creation, which is play, and which just because it has no *raison d'être* other than itself is the supreme motivating power in life.

Henry Miller (1891–1980), American novelist

Sleep lay upon the wilderness, it lay across the faces of nations, it lay like silence on the hearts of sleeping men; and low upon lowlands and high upon hills, flowed gently sleep, smooth-sliding sleep—sleep—sleep.

Thomas Wolfe (1900–1938), American novelist

[Idleness is] the occupation most becoming to a civilized man.

Théophile Gautier (1811–1872), French poet and novelist

Work is a dull thing; you cannot get away from that. The only agreeable existence is one of idleness, and that is not, unfortunately, always compatible with continuing to exist at all.

Dame Rosie Macaulay (1881–1958), English novelist

The men who do anything worth doing are just the men it is easiest to catch doing nothing.

Holbrook Jackson (1874–1948), English author

To be for one day entirely at leisure is to be for one day an immortal.

Chinese proverb

The right to laziness is one of the rights that sensible humanity will learn to consider as something self-evident. For the time being we are still in conflict with ourselves. We shun the truth. We look upon our laziness as degrading. We still stand in too much awe of ourselves to be able to find the right measure. Our mothers' voices still ring in our ears: "Have you done your lessons?"

Dr. Wilhelm Stekel (1868–1940), Austrian psychoanalyst

Someday is not a day of the week.
Anonymous

You know you're getting old when it takes too much effort to procrastinate.
Anonymous

You can discover more about a person in an hour of play than in a year of conversation.
Plato (429–347 B.C.), Greek philosopher

All paid jobs absorb and degrade the mind.
Aristotle (384–322 B.C.), Greek philosopher

I don't think necessity is the mother of invention. Invention, in my opinion, arises directly from idleness, possibly also from laziness—to save oneself trouble.
Dame Agatha Christie (1890–1976), English author

There are so many things that we wish we had done yesterday, so few that we feel like doing today.
Mignon McLaughlin (b. 1930), American writer

I do not participate in any sport with ambulances at the bottom of a hill.
Erma Bombeck (1927–1996), American writer and humorist

I think making love is the best form of exercise.
Cary Grant (1904–1996), English-born American film actor

[Bed is] a place of luxury for me. I would not exchange it for all the thrones in the world.
Napoleon Bonaparte (1769–1821), French emperor

[Bed is] a bundle of paradoxes; we go to it with reluctance, yet we quit it with regret; we make up our minds every night to leave it early, but we make up our bodies every morning to keep it late.
Charles Caleb Colton (1780–1832), English Anglican clergyman

The primary purpose of a liberal education is to make sure one's mind is a pleasant place in which to spend one's leisure.
Sydney J. Harris (1917–1986), American journalist and author

Idleness is not doing nothing. Idleness is *being free to do anything*.
Floyd Dell (1887–1969), American novelist and playwright

It was such a lovely day I thought it was a pity to get up.
W. Somerset Maugham (1874–1965), English novelist and playwright

My only solution for the problem of habitual accidents . . . is to stay in bed all day. Even then, there is always the chance you will fall out.
Robert Benchley (1889–1945), American writer and humorist

People are so busy lengthening their lives with exercise they don't have time to live them.
Jonathan Miller (b. 1934), English writer, performer, and director

I get my exercise acting as a pallbearer to my friends who exercise.
Chauncey Depew (1834–1928), American lawyer and businessman

Most of the evils of life arise from man's being unable to sit in a room.
Blaise Pascal (1623–1662), French mathematician, physicist, and theologian

How many inner resources one needs to tolerate a life of leisure without fatigue.
Natalie Clifford Barney (1876–1972), American-born French author

Leisure pastime in this country has become so complicated that it is now hard work . . . .We are not far from the time when a man after a hard weekend of leisure will go thankfully off to his job to unwind.
Russell Baker (b. 1925), American journalist and author

Overwork: *n.* A dangerous disorder affecting high public officials who want to go fishing.
Ambrose Bierce (1842–1914), American writer

Things have dropped from me. I have outlived certain desires; I have lost friends, some by death . . . others through sheer inability to cross the street.
Virginia Woolf (1882–1941), English author

Far from idleness being the root of all evil, it is rather only the true good.
Søren Kierkegaard (1813–1855), Danish philosopher

We seldom call anybody lazy, but such as we reckon inferior to us, and of whom we expect some service.
Bernard de Mandeville (1670–1733), Dutch-born English author

There is always time for a nap.
Suzy Becker (twentieth century), American writer and illustrator

[Idleness] does not consist in doing nothing, but in doing a great deal not recognized in the dogmatic formularies of the ruling classes.
Robert Louis Stevenson (1850–1894), Scottish writer

I believe every human has a finite number of heartbeats. I don't intend to waste any of mine running around.
Neil Armstrong (b. 1930), American astronaut

I don't jog. If I die I want to be sick.
Abe Lemons (twentieth century), American humorist

lust

lust

Sin: Lust

Definition: (lust), *n.* 1. uncontrolled or illicit sexual desire or appetite; lecherousness 2. A passionate or overmastering desire 3. a strong or excessive craving

See: lasciviousness; greediness; passion; aphrodisia; concupiscence; prurience; wantonness; erotism; sensuality; lechery; appetency; salaciousness; ardor; fervor; libido; intensity; amorality; infatuation; whorishness; intemperance; easy virtue; vice; lickerishness; fleshliness; lubricity; license; libertinism; dissoluteness; dissipation; voluptuousness; profligacy; goatishness; nymphomania; priapism; venery; harlotry; satyriasis; immorality; avidity; lewdness; carnality; promiscuity; wickedness;

corruption; iniquity; depravity; unchastity; smuttiness; pornography; indecency; seduction; obsession

See also: ache; covet; itch; need; long; pine; thirst; want; yearn; love; wish; crave; rut; pimp; pander; procure; fornicate; debauch; womanize; wench; deflower; fornicate; screw around; sleep around; hunger for; have a round eye; make the beast with two backs; be consumed by desire; be hot for; be unfaithful; be horny; be in heat; be turned on; be randy; be loose; be impure; be rakish

I don't know what I am dahlling. I've tried several varieties of sex. The conventional position makes me claustrophobic. And the others either give me a stiff neck or lockjaw.
Tallulah Bankhead (1903–1968), American actor

To seduce a woman famous for strict morals, religious fervor and the happiness of her marriage: What could possibly be more prestigious?
Christopher Hampton (b. 1946), English playwright

A man can have two, maybe three love affairs while he's married. After that it's cheating.
Yves Montand (1921–1991), Italian-born French actor and singer

A man can sleep around, no questions asked, but a woman who makes nineteen or twenty mistakes, she's a tramp.
Joan Rivers (b. 1933), American comedian and writer

When she raises her eyelids it's as if she were taking off all her clothes.
Colette (1873–1954), French writer

Men aren't attracted to me by my mind. They're attracted by what I don't mind.
Gypsy Rose Lee (1914–1970), American stripper, actor, and writer

Going to bed with a woman never hurt a ballplayer. It's staying up all night looking for them that does you in.
Casey Stengel (1890–1975), American baseball player and manager

Sex is one of nine reasons for reincarnation. The other eight are unimportant.
Henry Miller (1891–1980), American novelist

Whoever named it necking was a poor judge of anatomy.
Groucho Marx (1890–1977), American comedian

Certainly nothing is unnatural that is not physically impossible.
Richard Brinsley Sheridan (1751–1816), Irish-born English playwright

The only unnatural sex act is one which you cannot perform.
Alfred Kinsey (1894–1956), American biologist and sex researcher

If you believe there is a God, a God that made your body, and yet you think that you can do anything with that body that's dirty, then the fault lies with the manufacturer.
Lenny Bruce (1926–1966), American comedian

The good thing about masturbation is that you don't have to dress up for it.
Truman Capote (1924–1984), American novelist and playwright

Intercourse with a woman is sometimes a satisfactory substitute for masturbation. But it takes a lot of imagination to make it work.
Karl Kraus (1874–1936), Austrian journalist, poet, and playwright

Dancing is a perpendicular expression of a horizontal desire.
George Bernard Shaw (1856–1950), Irish playwright, author, and critic

A dress makes no sense unless it inspires men to want to take it off you.
Françoise Sagan (b. 1935), French novelist

All women's dresses are merely variations on the external struggle between the admitted desire to dress and the unadmitted desire to undress.
Lin Yutang (1895–1976), Chinese-born American writer

A woman is truly beautiful when she is naked and she knows it.
André Courreges (b. 1923), French fashion designer

Man's brains have transformed the earth and the sea, but sensuality remains what is was before the flood. Women; Wine; Noise.
William Bolitho (1891–1930), English journalist and author

Masturbation! The amazing availability of it!
James Joyce (1882–1941), Irish author

If I had as many love affairs as you have given me credit for, I would be speaking to you from a jar in the Harvard Medical School.
Frank Sinatra (b. 1915), American singer and actor

Dorothy Parker was told that a certain London actress had broken a leg. "How terrible," she said, "she must have done it sliding down a barrister."
As recounted by Clifton Fadiman (b. 1904), American author and editor

Last time I tried to make love to my wife nothing was happening, so I said to her, "What's the matter, you can't think of anybody else either?"
Rodney Dangerfield (b. 1922), American comedian and actor

Sex is nobody's business except the three people involved.
Anonymous

Lust is to the other passions what the nervous fluid is to life; it supports them all, lends strength to them all . . . ambition, cruelty, avarice, revenge, are all founded on lust.
Marquis de Sade (1740–1814), French author

Be advised by me, do not come to soon to the climax of your pleasure, but by skillful holding back, reach it gently . . . Do not, by setting too much sail, leave your mistress behind you; nor let her get too much in front of you. Row together towards the port. Voluptuousness reaches its greatest height when, overcome by it, lover and mistress are overcome at the same time. This ought to be your rule when there is no hurry and you are not compelled by fear of discovery to hasten your furtive pleasure. But if there is any danger in taking your time, then, bend to the oars, row with all your strength, and press your spurs in the thighs of your steed.

Ovid (43 B.C.–A.D. 17), Roman poet

There goes the good time that was had by all.

Bette Davis (1908–1989), American actor, remarking on a passing starlet

There are no chaste minds. Minds copulate wherever they meet.

Eric Hoffer (1902–1983), American author

There are few virtuous women who are not bored with their trade.

Duc François de la Rochefoucauld (1613–1680), French author

Brevity may be the soul of wit, but not when someone's saying "I love you." When someone's saying "I love you," he always ought to give a lot of details: Like, Why does he love you? And, How much does he love you? And, When and where did he first begin to love you? Favorable comparisons with all the other women he has ever loved are also welcome. And even though he insists it would take forever to count the ways in which he loves you, let him start counting.

Judith Viorst (b. 1935), American poet and journalist

In love affairs it is only the beginnings that are amusing. Therefore, you should start over again as soon as possible.

Marquise de Sévigné (1626–1696), French author

You may build castles in the air, and fume, and fret, and grow thin and lean, and pale and ugly, if you please. But I tell you, no man worth having is true to his wife, or can be true to his wife, or ever was, or will be so.

Sir John Vanbrugh (1664–1726), English playwright and architect

The pleasure is momentary, the position ridiculous and the expense damnable.

Lord Chesterfield (1694–1773), English statesman

It doesn't matter what you do in the bedroom as long as you don't do it in the street and frighten the horses.
Mrs. Patrick Campbell (1865–1940), English actor

You have to penetrate a woman's defenses. Getting into her head is a prerequisite to getting into her body.
Bob Guccione (b. 1930), American publisher

All really great lovers are articulate, and verbal seduction is the surest road to actual seduction.
Marya Mannes (1904–1990), American writer

I had prayed to you for chastity and said "Give me chastity and continence, but not yet." For I was afraid that you would answer my prayer at once and cure me too soon of the disease of lust, which I wanted satisfied, not quelled.
Saint Augustine (354–430), Church father and philosopher

There is no such thing as a life of passion any more than a continuous earthquake, or an eternal fever. Besides, who would ever *shave* themselves in such a state?
Lord Byron (1788–1824), English poet

She gave me a smile I could feel in my hip pocket.
Raymond Chandler (1888–1959), American author

I am happy now that Charles calls on my bedchamber less frequently than of old. As it is, I now endure but two calls a week and when I hear his steps outside my door I lie down on my bed, close my eyes, open my legs and think of England.
Second Baron Hillingdon

My life with girls has ended, though til lately I was up to it and soldiered on not ingloriously; now on this wall will hang my weapons and my lyre, discharged from the war.
Horace (65–68 B.C.), Roman lyric poet

Someone asked Sophocles, "How do you feel now about sex? Are you still able to have a woman?" He replied, "Hush, man; most glad indeed I am to be rid of it all, as though I had escaped from a mad and savage master."
Plato (429–347 B.C.), Greek philosopher

The amount of women in London who flirt with their own husbands is perfectly scandalous. It looks so bad. It is simply washing one's clean linen in public.
Oscar Wilde (1854–1900), Irish poet, wit, and playwright

Once: a philosopher; twice: a pervert!
Voltaire (1694–1778), French author, turning down an invitation to an orgy, having gone to his first one the evening before

I tend to believe that cricket is the greatest thing God created on earth . . . certainly greater than sex, although sex isn't too bad either.
Harold Pinter (b. 1930), English playwright

A man marries to have a home, but also because he doesn't want to be bothered with sex and all that sort of thing.
W. Somerset Maugham (1874–1965), English novelist and playwright

Of the seven deadly sins, Lust is the only one about which all mankind (with very few exceptions) knows something from experience. People own to this awkward fact in general, but not in particular. Even in an age which prides itself on being "outspoken," people usually remain careful to avoid any suggestion that they themselves are prone to unlawful passions, or to the extravaganza which goes with erotic feelings. Hence a great measure of falsification in most writing and talk on the subject, even in the most advanced society. But to say, "Lust is a vice I cannot understand" would be to overdo it; it would not wash in any society at all. Hence the flight from hypocrisy to coyness. All men are potentially lustful, and a huge proportion are so in practice.
Christopher Sykes (1907–1986), English author and editor

The daughter-in-law of Pythagoras said that a woman who goes to bed with a man ought to lay aside her modesty with her skirt, and put in on again with her petticoat.
Michel Eyquem de Montaigne (1533–1592), French essayist

My response . . . was . . . to evolve my fantasy of the Zipless Fuck . . . Zipless because when you come together zippers fall away like petals.
Erica Jong (b. 1942), American poet and novelist

When Eve ate this particular apple, she became aware of her own womanhood, mentally. And mentally she began to experiment with it. She has been experimenting ever since. So has man. To the rage and horror of both of them.
D. H. Lawrence (1885–1930), English novelist

The reproduction of mankind is a great marvel and mystery. Had God consulted me in the matter, I should have advised him to continue the generation of the species by fashioning them of clay.
Martin Luther (1483–1546), German religious reformer

What most men desire is a virgin who is a whore.
Edward Dahlberg (1900–1977), American writer

Lust's passion will be served; it demands, it militates, it tyrannizes.
Marquis de Sade (1740–1814), French author

A gentleman doesn't pounce. . . . he glides. If a woman sits on a piece of furniture which permits your sitting beside her, you are free to regard this as an invitation, though not an unequivocal one.
Quentin Crisp (b. 1908), English author

One can find two women who have never had one love affair, but it is rare indeed to find any who have had only one.

1680), French author

Many a man has fallen in love with a girl in light so dim he would not have chosen a suit by it.
Maurice Chevalier (1888–1972), French actor and singer

Chastity is no more a virtue than malnutrition.
Alex Comfort (b. 1920), English physician, writer, and poet

A man of any age can convince himself that a woman's thighs are altar rails and that her passion is the hosanna of virtuous love rather than the wanton tumult of nerve endings.
Ben Hecht (1894–1964), American author

The art of procreation and the members employed therein are so repulsive, that if it were not for the beauty of the faces, the adornments of the actors, and the pent-up impulse, nature would lose the human species.
Leonardo da Vinci (1452–1519), Italian painter, sculptor, architect, engineer, and scientist

When I consider the absurd titillations of [love], the brainless motions it excites, the countenance inflamed with fury, and cruelty doing its sweetest effects; the grave, solemn entranced air in an action down right silly, the supreme moment bathed, like pain, in sighing and fainting—I then believe, with Plato, that the gods made men for their sport.
Michel Eyquem de Montaigne (1533–1592), French essayist

When lust, by unchaste looks, loose gestures, and foul talk, but most by lewd and lavish acts of sin, lets in defilement to the inward parts, the soul grows clotted by contagion, embodies and imbrutes till she quite loses the divine property of her first being.
John Milton (1608–1674), English poet

An enemy to whom you show kindness becomes your friend, excepting lust, the indulgence of which increases its enmity.
Shaikh Saadi (1184?–1291), Persian poet

Lust is an enemy to the purse, a foe to the person, a canker to the mind, a corrosive to the conscience, a weakness of the wit, a besotter of the senses, and, finally, a mortal bane to all the body.
Pliny the Elder (23–79), Roman scholar

Lust is, of all the frailties of our nature, what most we ought to fear; the headstrong beast rushes along impatient of the course; nor hears the rider's call, nor feels the rein.
Nicholas Rowe (1674–1718), English poet and playwright

[Lust is when] the loin lies down with the limb.
Conrad Aiken (1889–1973), American poet, critic, and author

Men . . . show their masculinity throughout their boyhood by the way they make friends with men, and the delight they take in lying beside them and being taken in their arms. And these are the most hopeful of the nation's youth, for theirs is the most virile constitution.
Plato (429–347 B.C.), Greek philosopher

'Tis the Devil inspires this evanescent ardor, in order to divert the parties f rom prayer.
Martin Luther (1483–1546), German religious reformer

Sex touches the heavens only when it simultaneously touches the gutter and the mud.
George Jean Nathan (1882–1958), American editor, author, and critic

It is not enough to conquer; one must know how to seduce.
Voltaire (1694–1778), French author

Women can always be caught; that's the first rule of the game.
Ovid (43 B.C.–A.D. 17), Roman poet

To win a woman in the first place one must please her, then undress her, and then somehow get her clothes back on her. Finally, so that she will allow you to leave her, you've got to annoy her.
Jean Giraudoux (1882–1944), French playwright, novelist, essayist, and diplomat

The truly erotic sensibility, in evoking the image of woman, never omits to clothe it. The robing and disrobing: That is the true traffic of love.
Antonio Machado (1875–1939), Spanish poet

Much contention and strife will arise in that house where the wife shall get up dissatisfied with her husband.
Shaikh Saadi (1184?–1291), Persian poet

You know women as well as I do. They are only willing when you compel them, but after that they're as enthusiastic as you are.

Jean Giraudoux (1882–1944), French playwright, novelist, essayist, and diplomat

The sages figured lust in the form of a satyr; of shape, part human, part bestial; to signify that the followers of it prostitute the reason of a man to pursue the appetites of a beast.

Richard Steele (1672–1729), English essayist and playwright

A kiss is a lovely trick designed by nature to stop speech when words become superfluous.

Ingrid Bergman (1915–1982), Swedish-born American actress

The kiss originated when the first male reptile licked the first female reptile, implying in a subtle, complimentary way that she was as succulent as the small reptile he had for dinner the night before.

F. Scott Fitzgerald (1896–1940), American author

Women should be obscene and not heard.

Groucho Marx (1895–1977), American film and television comedian

My reaction to porno films is as follows: After the first ten minutes, I want to go home and screw. After the first twenty minutes, I never want to screw again for as long as I live.

Erica Jong (b. 1942), American poet and novelist

It was a blonde. A blonde to make a bishop kick a hole in a stained glass window.

Raymond Chandler (1888–1959), American author

I don't think there are any men who are faithful to their wives.

Jacqueline Kennedy Onassis (1929–1994), American first lady to American president John F. Kennedy (1917–1963)

Eighty percent of married men cheat in America. The rest cheat in Europe.

Jackie Mason (b. 1931), American comedian

Husbands are chiefly good lovers when they are betraying their wives.

Marilyn Monroe (1926–1962), American film star

I kissed my first girl and smoked my first cigarette on the same day. I haven't had time for tobacco since.

Arturo Toscanini (1867–1957), Italian conductor

For the preservation of chastity, an empty and rumbling stomach and fevered lungs are indispensable.

Saint Jerome (340?–420), Latin scholar

I'm against group sex because I wouldn't know where to put my elbows.

Martin Cruz Smith (b. 1942), American author

The man and woman make love, attain climax, fall separate. Then she whispers "I'll tell you who I was thinking of if you tell me who you were thinking of." Like most sex jokes the origins of the pleasant exchange are obscure. But whatever the source, it seldom fails to evoke an awful recognition.

Gore Vidal (b. 1925), American novelist and playwright

A woman's a woman until the day she dies, but a man's only a man as long as he can.

Moms Mabley (1894–1975), American comedian

Familiarity breeds attempt.

Goodman Ace (1899–1982), American humorist

Woman is: Finally screwing and your groin and buttocks and thighs ache like hell and you're all wet and maybe bloody and it wasn't like a Hollywood movie at all but Jesus at least you're not a virgin any more but is this what it's all about? And meanwhile, he's asking "Did you come?"

Robin Morgan (b. 1941), American feminist author

It is possible that blondes also prefer gentlemen.

Mamie Van Doren (b. 1933), American actor, on Warren Beatty

It's so much better to desire than to have. The moment of desire is the most extraordinary moment. The moment of desire, when you *know* something is going to happen—that's the most exalting.

Anouk Aimee (b. 1932), French actress

In my sex fantasy, nobody ever loves me for my mind.

Nora Ephron (b. 1941), American author, screenwriter, and director

How love the limb-loosener sweeps me away.

Sappho (seventh century B.C.), Greek poet

You can remember the second and the third and the fourth time, but there's no time like the first. It's always there.
Shelagh Delaney (b. 1939), English playwright

I often think that a slightly exposed shoulder emerging from a long satin nightgown packed more sex than two naked bodies in bed.
Bette Davis (1908–1989), American actor

The only sin passion can commit is to be joyless.
Dorothy Sayers (1893–1957), English writer

Sex hasn't been the same since women started enjoying it.
Lewis Grizzard (1946–1994), American writer and humorist

It is naive in the extreme for women to expect to be regarded as equals by men . . . so long as they persist in a subhuman (i.e., animal-like) behavior during sexual intercourse. I'm referring . . . to the outlandish *panting, gasping, moaning, sobbing, writhing, scratching, biting, screaming* conniptions, and the seemingly invariable *"Oh my God . . . Oh my God . . . Oh my God"* all so predictably integral to pre-, post-, and orgasmic stages of intercourse.
Terry Southern (b. 1926), American author

Your idea of fidelity is not having more than one man in bed at the same time.
Dirk Bogarde (b. 1920), English actor and novelist

I am a strict monogamist: It is twenty years since I last went to bed with two women at once, and then I was in my cups and not myself.
H. L. Mencken (1880–1956), American satirist and editor

A Code of Honor: Never approach a friend's girlfriend or wife with mischief as your goal. There are just too many women in the world to justify that sort of dishonorable behavior. Unless she's *really* attractive.
Bruce J. Friedman (b. 1930), American author

I love Mickey Mouse more than any woman I've ever known.
Walt Disney (1901–1966), American film producer

I tell the women that the face is my experience and the hands are my soul—anything to get those panties down.
Charles Bukowski (1920–1994), American author

Whatever else can be said about sex, it cannot be called a dignified performance.
Helen Lawrenson (1907–1982), American editor and author

There are a number of mechanical devices which increase sexual arousal, particularly in women. Chief among these is the Mercedes-Benz 380SL convertible.
P. J. O'Rourke (b. 1947), American writer and humorist

A man has missed something if he has never woken up in an anonymous bed beside a face he'll never see again, and if he has never left a brothel at dawn feeling like throwing himself into the river out of sheer disgust with life.
Gustave Flaubert (1821–1880), French novelist

Blondes have the hottest kisses. Redheads are fair-to-middling torrid, and brunettes are the frigidest of all. It's something to do with hormones, no doubt.
Ronald Reagan (b. 1911), American actor and fortieth president

Caroline of Brunswick was the wife of King George IV of England and at her divorce trial in 1820 before the house of lords, various salacious details of her behavior on her foreign travels were produced in evidence against her. One line of inquiry concerned her conduct with the dey (governor) of Algiers. The chief justice, Lord Norbury, remarked, "She was happy as the dey was long."
As reported by Clifton Fadiman (b. 1904), American author and editor

Seamed stockings aren't subtle but they certainly do the job. You shouldn't wear them out when out with someone you're not prepared to sleep with, since their presence is tantamount to saying, "Hi there, big fellow, please rip my clothes off at your earliest opportunity." If you really want your escort paralytic with lust, stop frequently to adjust the seams.
Cynthia Heimel (b. 1947), American writer

I am over-run, jungled in my bed, I am infested with a menagerie of desires; my heart is eaten by a dove, a cat scrambles in the cave of my sex, hounds in my head obey a whipmaster who cries nothing but havoc as the hours test my endurance with an accumulation of tortures.
Elizabeth Smart (1913–1986), Canadian author and poet

The light covering of flesh was so transmuted with ecstasy that earthly passion became a heavenly embrace of white, fiery flame.
Isadora Duncan (1878–1927), American dancer

Sometimes in my dreams there are women. When such dreams happen, immediately I remember: "I am a monk."
Dalai Lama (b. 1935), temporal and spiritual leader of Tibet

Unless there's some emotional tie, I'd rather play tennis.
Bianca Jagger (b. 1945), actress

Barbara Stanwyck is my favorite. My God, I could just sit and dream of being married to her, having a little cottage out in the hills, vines around the door. I'd come home from the office tired and weary, and I'd be met by Barbara, walking through the door holding an apple pie she had cooked herself. And wearing no drawers.
Herbert J. Mankiewicz (1897–1953), American screenwriter and journalist

There is nothing wrong with going to bed with people of your own sex . . . . People should be very free with sex, they should draw the line at goats.
Elton John (b. 1947), English rock singer

All of my sexual experiences when I was young were with girls. I mean, we didn't have those sleep-over parties for nothing. I think that's really normal: same-sex experimentation. You get really curious, and there's your girl-friend, and she's spending the night with you, and it happens.
Madonna (b. 1958), American pop singer and actor

During sex I fantasize that I'm someone else.
Richard Lewis (b. 1947), American comedian and actor

No woman has ever slept with me too soon. . . . I've always found promiscuous women interesting. I suspect I would have been promiscuous if I'd been a woman. I certainly have been as a man.
Norman Mailer (b. 1923), American writer

When I have sex it takes four minutes. And that includes dinner and a show.
Gilbert Gottfried (b. 1955), American comedian

Winning a Grammy sure helped me get laid.
Bonnie Raitt (b. 1949), American singer

I can't get to sleep unless I've had a lay.
John F. Kennedy (1917–1963), thirty-fifth American president

I've slept with more women by accident than John Kennedy has slept with on purpose.

Lyndon Baines Johnson (1908–1973), thirty-sixth American president

The ability to enjoy your sex life is central. I don't give a shit about anything else. My obsession is total. What else is there to live for?

Dudley Moore (b. 1935), English actor and comedian

Only the brute is really potent. Sexuality is the lyricism of the masses.

Charles Baudelaire (1821–1867), French poet

Girls marry for "love." Boys marry because of a chronic irritation that causes them to gravitate in the direction of objects with certain curvilinear properties.

Ashley Montague (b. 1905), American anthropologist

I regret to say that we of the FBI are powerless to act in cases of oral-genital intimacy, unless it has in some way obstructed interstate commerce.

J. Edgar Hoover (1895–1972), director of the FBI

I sleep with men and with women. I am neither queer nor not queer, nor am I bisexual.

Allen Ginsberg (b. 1926), American poet

No matter which sex I went to bed with, I never smoked on the street.

Florence King (b. 1936), American author

I think any man in business would be foolish to fool around with his secretary. If it's somebody else's secretary, fine.

Senator Barry Goldwater (b. 1909), American politician

I like to wake up each morning feeling a new man.

Jean Harlow (1911–1937), American film actor

And then I asked him with my eyes to ask again yes and then he asked me would I yes to say yes my mountain flower and first I put my arms around him yes and drew him down to me so he could feel my breasts all perfume yes and his heart was going like mad and yes I said yes I will Yes.

James Joyce (1882–1941), Irish author

I don't like to admit it, but if a girl baited her trap with sex, she'd catch me every time—and it's unlikely this will ever cease to work.

Willie Nelson (b. 1933), American singer

I may not be a great actress but I've become the greatest at screen orgasms. Ten seconds of heavy breathing, roll your head from side to side, simulate a slight asthma attack, and die a little.

Candice Bergen (b. 1946), American actor

I like making love myself and I can make love for about *three minutes*. Three minutes of serious fucking and I need eight hours sleep, and a bowl of Wheaties.

Richard Pryor (b. 1940), American comedian and actor

After being alive, the next hardest work is sex. . . . Some people *get* energy from sex, and some people *lose* energy from sex. I have found that it's too much work. But if you have the time for it, and if you need the exercise—then you should do it.

Andy Warhol (1927–1987), American painter, graphic artist, and filmmaker

I was asked if my first sexual experience was homosexual or heterosexual. I said I was too polite to ask.

Gore Vidal (b. 1925), American novelist and playwright

What I say is that the supreme and singular joy of making love resides in the certainty of doing evil.

Charles Baudelaire (1821–1867), French poet

There has been another high-flown debate in the House of Lords about suggested (idiotic) amendments to the Homosexual Bill, in the course of which Lord Montgomery announced that homosexuality between men was the most abominable and beastly act that any human being could commit! It, in his mind, apparently compares unfavorably with disembowelling, torturing, gas chambers and brutal murder. It is inconceivable that a man of his eminence and achievements could make such a statement. The poor old sod must be gaga.

Noël Coward (1899–1973), English actor and playwright

It is called in our schools "beastliness," and this is about the best name for it . . . should it become a habit it quickly destroys both health and spirits; he becomes feeble in body and mind, and often ends in a lunatic asylum.

Robert Baden-Powell (1857–1941), English soldier and founder of the Boy Scouts

All this talk about sex, all this worry about sex—big deal. The sun makes me happy. I eat a good fish, it makes me happy. I sleep with a good man, he makes me happy.

Melina Mercouri (1923–1994), Greek actor and politician

An old friend and mentor, Sir Clifford Norton, told me about sex education in Rugby before the First World War. The headmaster, who must have been an enlightened man, summoned all the boys who had reached the age of puberty to his study and, after reassuring himself that the door was firmly secured, made the following brief announcement: "If you touch it, it will fall off."

Sir Peter Ustinov (b. 1921), English playwright, actor, director, and writer

Erotic life is the spindle on which the earth turns.

Octavio Paz (b. 1914), Mexican poet, essayist, social philosopher, and critic

If we love we must not live as other men and women do—I cannot brook the wolfsbane of fashion and foppery and tattle. You must be mine to die upon the rack if I want you . . . Good bye! I kiss you—O the torments.

John Keats (1795–1821), English poet

The advantages are manifold. Not only will the purity of the virgin be maintained, but the fidelity of the wife exacted. The husband will leave the wife without fear that his honour will be outraged and his affections estranged.

A French merchandising house advertising The Girdle of Chastity, 1880

I like young girls. Their stories are shorter.

Thomas McGuane (b. 1939), American novelist

For when I glance at you even an instant, I can no longer utter a word: my tongue thickens to a lump, and beneath my skin breaks out a subtle fire: my eyes are blind, my ears filled with humming, and sweat streams down my body, I am seized by a sudden shuddering; I turn greener than grass, and in a moment more, I feel I shall die.

Sappho (seventh century B.C.), Greek poet

When a woman is awakened, when she gets the man she wants, she is amazing, amazing . . . sensuality is a whole separate world. Love is like a mine. You go deeper and deeper. There are passages, caves, whole strata. You discover entire geological eras.

Christopher Isherwood (1904–1986), English playwright and author

All witchcraft comes from carnal lust which in women is insatiable.

Jacob Sprenger and Hendrich Kramer (fifteenth century), German Dominican monks

All men and women woo me. There is a fragrance in their breath.

Henry David Thoreau (1817–1862), American author and Naturalist

How a man must hug, and dandle, and kittle, and play a hundred little tricks with his bed-fellow when he is disposed to make that use of her that nature designed for her.

Desiderius Erasmus (1466?–1536), Dutch scholar

I came out of the closet at Columbia in 1946. The first person I told about it was Kerouac, 'cause I was in love with him. He was staying in my room up in the bed, and I was sleeping on a pallet on the floor. I said, "Jack, you know, I love you, and I want to sleep with you, and I really like men." And he said, "Oooooh, no . . ."

Allen Ginsberg (b. 1926), American poet

Do you know that in ancient Greek there was no word for homosexuality? Because there is just . . . to be *sexual*. One is not this or that, one is *sexual*.

Luchino Visconti (1906–1976), Italian film director

Her sex power . . . hid in her eyes like a Sicilian bandit.

Saul Bellow (b. 1915), Canadian-born American author

Orgasm is like the tickling feeling you get inside your nose before you sneeze.

Children's sex education manual, 1972

I believe that sex is the most beautiful, natural, and wholesome thing that money can buy.

Steve Martin (b. 1945), American comedian, actor, and playwright

I wouldn't trust my husband with a young woman for five minutes, and he's been dead for twenty-five years.

Mother of Irish playwright Brendan Behan

The biggest, strongest, most powerful men can be reduced by sex to imps.

Isaac Bashevis Singer (1904–1991), Yiddish novelist, critic, and journalist

I had often looked at my penis and thought, "*You moron*."

Paul Theroux (b. 1941), American novelist and travel writer

The important thing in acting is to be able to laugh and cry. If I have to cry, I think of my sex life. If I have to laugh, I think of my sex life.

Glenda Jackson (b. 1936), English actor

I'd rather hit than have sex.

Reggie Jackson (b. 1946), American baseball player

The only men who are too young are the ones who write love letters in crayon, wear pajamas with feet, or fly for half fare.

Phyllis Diller (b. 1917), American comedian and actor

Anyone who knows Dan Quayle knows that he would rather play golf than have sex any day.

Marilyn Quayle (b. 1949), wife of Dan Quayle, vice president to George Bush, forty-first American president

Lust is repulsive. It shows as a beast. Desire is so compelling, so like true love to the inexperienced, so related to the glamour and poetry of life, that its poison is the more deadly. . . . Desire passes with satiety. Love includes but sublimates desire. Love shines more brightly and in varying lights as desire passes into its spiritual fulfillments.

Committee on Marriage and Home, Federal Council of Churches of Christ in America, 1929

There has never been a woman yet in the world who wouldn't have given the top of the milk-jug to some man, if she had met the right one.

Ascribed to Lady Wilde, mother of Irish writer Oscar Wilde (1854–1900)

A reputation for chastity is necessary to a woman. Chastity itself is also sometimes useful.

Anonymous

Silk was invented so that women could go naked in clothes.

Muhammad (570–632), founder of Islam

Complete nudity is never permitted. This includes nudity in fact or in silhouette, or any lecherous or licentious notice thereof by other characters in the pictures.

A Code to Govern the Making of Motion and Talking Pictures by the Motion Picture Producers and Distributors of America, Inc., March 31, 1930

These, it is true, are abstinent; but from all that they do the bitch of sensuality looks out with envious eyes.

Friedrich Nietzsche (1844–1900), German philosopher and poet

An unattempted woman cannot boast of her chastity.

Michel Eyquem de Montaigne (1533–1592), French essayist

The prettiest dresses are worn to be taken off.

Jean Cocteau (1889–1963), French poet, novelist, and director

At the climax, you were lit up with a quiet ecstasy, which enveloped your blessed body in a supernatural nimbus, like a cloak that you pierced with your head and feet.

Jean Genet (1910–1986), French playwright and novelist

Although they have good-looking women, they pay very little attention to them, but are really crazy about having sex with men. They are accustomed to sleep on the ground on animal skins and roll around with male bed-mates on both sides. Heedless of their own dignity, they abandon without a qualm the bloom of their bodies to others. And the most incredible thing is that they don't think this is shameful. But when they proposition someone, they consider it dishonorable if he doesn't accept the offer!

Diodorus Siculus (first century B.C.), Roman historian, commenting on the homosexuality among Celtic males of the period

Even in civilized mankind faint traces of monogamous instinct can be perceived.

Bertrand Russell (1872–1970), English philosopher

I am *Tarzan* of the *Apes*. I want you. I am yours. You are mine.

Edgar Rice Burroughs (1875–1950), American novelist

My love was so hot as mighty nigh to burst my boilers.

Davy Crockett (1786–1836), American backwoodsman

The duration of passion is proportionate with the original resistance of the woman.

Honoré de Balzac (1799–1850), French novelist

I will find you twenty lascivious turtles ere one chaste man.

William Shakespeare (1564–1616), English playwright and poet

I don't know whether it's normal or not, but sex has always been something that I take seriously. I would put it higher than tennis on my list of constructive things to do.

Art Buchwald (b. 1925), American humorist

There is nothing like early promiscuous sex for dispelling life's bright mysterious expectations.

Iris Murdoch (b. 1919), Irish-born English novelist

How true is the saying, "It is impossible to live with the tormentors [women], impossible to live without them."

Aristophanes (448?–380? B.C.), Greek playwright and poet

The sexual act cannot be reduced to a chapter on hygienics; it is an exciting, dark, sinful, diabolical experience. Sex is a black tarantula and sex without religion is like an egg without salt. . . . Sex multiplies the possibilities of desire.

Luis Buñuel (1900–1983), Spanish filmmaker

The natural rhythm of human life is routine punctuated by orgies.

Aldous Huxley (1894–1963), English author

The pleasure of the act of love is gross and brief and brings loathing after it.
Gaius Petronius (first century A.D.), probable author of the *Satyricon*

Some say that when pleasure is the chief motive of the marriage act it is a mortal sin; that when it is an indirect motive it is a venial sin; and that when it spurns the pleasure altogether, and is displeasing, it is wholly void of venial sin; so that it would be a mortal sin to take pleasure when it is offered, but that perfection requires one to detest it. But this is impossible since . . . the same judgment applies to pleasure as to action, because pleasure in a good action is good, and in an evil action, evil; therefore as the marriage act is not evil in itself, neither will it be always a mortal sin to seek pleasure therein.
Saint Thomas Aquinas (1224–1274), Italian Dominican monk and theologian

May my enemies love women.
May my friends delight in boys.
Sextus Propertius (50?–15? B.C.), Roman poet

I've looked on a lot of women with lust. I've committed adultery in my heart many times. This is something God recognizes I will do—and I have done it—and God forgives me for it.
Jimmy Carter (b. 1924), thirty-ninth A merican president

Thunder and lightning, wars, fires, plagues, have not done that mischief to mankind as this burning lust, this brutish passion.
Robert Burton (1577–1640), English clergyman and author

How do you like them? Like a pear, a lemon, *a la Montegolfiere*, half an apple, or a cantaloupe? Go on, choose, don't be embarrassed. You thought they didn't exist any longer, that they were all over with, absolutely done for. . . . If you don't mind, Madame, let's bring things up to date. They exist, and persist, however criticized and persecuted they may be.
Colette (1873–1954), French writer, on breasts

Pursuit and seduction are the essence of sexuality. It's part of the sizzle.
Camille Paglia (b. 1947), American author, critic, and educator

I know the nature of women:
When you want to, they don't want to;
And when you don't want to, they
desire exceedingly.
Terence (186?–159 B.C.), Roman poet

Adultery is in your heart not only when you look with excessive sexual zeal at a woman who is not your wife, but also if you look in the same manner at your wife.
Pope John Paul II (b. 1920)

At noon I observed a bevy of nude native young ladies bathing in the sea, and I went down and sat on their clothes to keep them from being stolen.
Mark Twain (1835–1910), American writer, while in Hawaii

To me inspiration and creativity come only when I have abstained from a woman for a longish period. When, with passion, I have emptied my fluid into a woman until I am pumped dry, then inspiration shuns me . . . .
Frédéric Chopin (1810–1849), Polish-born French composer

It's only horny people who shoot people. I mean, you never feel aggressive after you've just gotten laid.
Ted Turner (b. 1938), American entertainment executive

When turkeys mate, they think of swans.
Johnny Carson (b. 1925), American comedian

My attitude toward men who mess around is simple: If you find them, kill them.
Loretta Lynn (b. 1935), American singer

First in war, first in peace, first in the pants of his countrywomen.
Woodrow Wilson (1856–1924), twenty-eighth American president, on George Washington

You never know a guy until you've tried him in bed. You know more about a guy in one night in bed than you do in months of conversation. In the sack, they can't cheat.
Edith Piaf (1915–1963), French singer

For a man to have sex with another man is to become doubly a man.
Jean Genet (1910–1986), French playwright and novelist

I caught sight of a splendid Misses. She had handkerchiefs and kisses. She had eyes and yellow shoes she had everything to choose and she chose me. In passing through France she wore a Chinese hat and so did I. In looking at the sun she read a map. And so did I. In eating fish and pork she just grew fat. And so did I. In loving a blue sea she had a pain. And so did I. In loving me she of necessity thought first. And so did I. How prettily we swim. Not in water. Not on land. But in love.
Gertrude Stein (1874–1946), American author

If you were married to Marilyn Monroe—you'd cheat with some ugly girl.
George Burns (1896–1996), American comedian and actor

It's better to copulate than never.
Robert Heinlein (1907–1988), American writer

Sex for a fat man is much ado about puffing.

Jackie Gleason (1916–1987), American comedian and actor

I tried phone sex and it gave me an ear infection.

Richard Lewis (b. 1943), American comedian and actor

It is a gentlemen's first duty to remember in the morning who it was he took to bed with him.

Dorothy Sayers (1893–1957), English author

[Sex is] like air . . . not important until you're not getting any.

Debbie Reynolds (b. 1932), American actor

Sex is like money; only too much is enough.

John Updike (b. 1932), American author and critic

The Englishman can get along without sex quite perfectly so long as he can pretend that it isn't sex but something else.

James Agate (1877–1947), English drama critic

If you live in rock and roll, as I do, you see the reality of sex, of male lust and women being aroused by male lust. It attracts women. It doesn't repel them.

Camille Paglia (b. 1947), American author, critic, and educator

I didn't like it like that. Not against the bricks or hunkering in somebody's car. I wanted it come undone like gold thread, like a tent full of birds.

Sandra Cisneros (b. 1954), Mexican-American writer, poet, and educator

Power is the great aphrodisiac.

Henry Kissinger (b. 1923), American secretary of state

Henry's idea of sex is to slow the car down to thirty miles an hour when he drops you off at the door.

Barbara Howar (b. 1934), American television correspondent and writer, on Henry Kissinger

License my roving hands, and let
them go
Before, behind, between, above, below.

John Donne (1573–1631), English poet

I date men and I date women. What Woody Allen said was true. Say what you will about bisexuality, you have a fifty percent better chance of finding a date on Saturday night.

David Geffen (b. 1943), American entertainment executive

Okay, okay. If you're asking am I one, I'll go that route—good public relations. If it's good enough for Gore Vidal and Elton John, it's good enough for me. I am bisexual, happy and proud. A woman in every bed . . . and a man, too. Satisfied?

Rock Hudson (1925–1985), American actor

If a woman hasn't got a tiny streak of the harlot in her, she's a dry stick.

D. H. Lawrence (1885–1930), English novelist

All I wanted was a man
With a single heart . . .
Not somebody always after wriggling
fish
With his bamboo rod.

Chuo Wen-Chun (179–117 B.C.), Chinese poet

If you should take your wife in adultery, you may with impunity put her to death without a trial; but if you should commit adultery or indecency, she must not presume to lay a finger on you, not does the law allow it.

Cato the Elder (234–149 B.C.), Roman statesman

Making love? It's a communion with a woman. The bed is the holy table. There I find passion—and purification.

Omar Sharif (b. 1932), Egyptian actor

If any of your women be guilty of whoredom, then bring your witnesses against them from among themselves; and if they bear witness to the fact, shut them up within their houses till death release them, or God make some way for them.

The Koran, Chapter IV

Many the girls and women I have loved, both lad and man; many the boys and men I have loved, both lad and man.

Unknown German monk (1150)

I have made love to 10,000 women since I was 13 (and a half). It wasn't in any way a vice. I've no sexual vices. But I needed to communicate.

Georges Simenon (1903–1989), Belgian novelist

That's correct—20,000 different ladies. At my age that equals out to having sex with 1.2 women a day, every day since I was fifteen.

Wilt Chamberlain (b. 1936), American basketball player

Lolita, light of my life, fire of my loins. My sin, my soul. Lo-lee-ta: the tip of the tongue taking a trip of three steps down the palate to tap, at three, on the teeth. Lo. Lee. Ta.

Vladimir Nabokov (1899–1977), Russian-born American novelist and poet

God hath prepared . . . a little coronet or special reward (extraordinary and beside the great crown of all faithful souls) for those who have not defiled themselves with women.

Jeremy Taylor (1613–1667), English churchman and writer

To see you naked is to recall the Earth.

Federico García Lorca (1898–1936), Spanish poet and playwright

The trouble with life is that there are so many beautiful women and so little time.

John Barrymore (1882–1942), American actor

'Tisn't beauty, so to speak, nor good talk necessarily. It's just *it*. Some women'll stay in a man's memory if they once walked down a street.

Rudyard Kipling (1865–1936), English author

Index

INDEX